W9-BXW-154

LIVE AN EXTREME LIFE!

Losing the Weight and Gaining My Purpose

"With Bob, this transformation is for good. Now, not to say he won't ever struggle, because we are all human, and life is a series of struggles and opportunities for growth. But Bob knows the secret behind transformation now. He can't un-know it. He grasped onto the secrets of true transformation—not just the numbers game on the scale. Simply put, Bob gets it."

~HEIDI POWELL, Transformation Specialist, *Extreme Weight Loss*

"Bob's story has stuck with me ever since watching it on Season 3 of *Extreme Weight Loss*. Yes, his physical transformation was simply beyond words, but knowing how he would inspire countless others who can relate to his past struggles is the best part. The way he has embraced this lifestyle change with his C.L.I.F. mentality will speak to so many others who will find the motivation and inspiration to follow in his footsteps."

~DREW MANNING, Fitness Celebrity/Health and Wellness Coach

"Bob was going to be a force to be reckoned with. Bob ended up tearing his ACL during camp but continued to work harder than anyone on the show. This, of course, inspired all of us to push ourselves and work to our maximum potential. I told myself, 'If I have two good knees and he is down one, I have zero excuses.' I still couldn't keep up with him. He is such an amazing athlete and person, and the perfect person to have by your side when you're going through the hardest year of your life. Bob is always positive and honest, and he is the brother I never had. I'm so proud of what he was able to accomplish and even prouder of the person he has become. I look up to Bob and love him and his family dearly."

~MEHRBOD MOHAMMADI, Season 3, *Extreme Weight Loss*

"Bob is a person with a true positive character. We bonded on the show due to us having knee issues, going to physical therapy, and working out together. During that time, I learned how truly amazing Bob is. He is not only an athlete, but he is a man with an extraordinary heart. His character speaks for itself. He is genuine, honest, loyal, dedicated, hardworking, and straightforward. Bob is a tell-it-as-it-is person."

~CASSANDRA DUMAS, Season 3, *Extreme Weight Loss*

"I was so encouraged by the message Bob Brenner recently delivered at my church, Legacy Christian in Menomonee Falls, Wisconsin. The week he delivered his message, I was right in the middle of leading a women's Bible Study, 'Made to Crave,' about craving God more than food. His message paralleled so much of what we were learning, and I know my fellow 'Jesus Girls' felt the same encouragement and empowerment as I did in hearing Bob's message. The transformation Bob shared with us was so much more than just a weight loss journey. It is a complete transformation of becoming the man God created him to be."

~FELICIA FROSCHMAYER, Christian Women's Leader

"Bob's true integrity shone, as I had expected from my previous encounter, when he presented his life journey, specifically, the poor choices he had made because of his overcommitment to meaningless activity. He discussed thresholds he had passed, where he believed the point of no return had been crossed, as well as monumental challenges he overcame by finally making the correct commitments in life. He shared his true loves in life and how he held these people close to him during his trials while on a weight loss challenge. Faith and integrity were crucial in his quest as he faced his abyss. In all, our students learned to climb their own C.L.I.F. (Commitment, Love, Integrity, and Faith)."

~STACY ROZMARYNOWSKI, Advisory
Instructor, Kohler Public Schools

Live an Extreme Life!

Losing the Weight and Gaining My Purpose

Bob Brenner

with Reji Laberje

Foreword by Chris Powell

Copyright © 2014 by Bob Brenner

ALL RIGHTS RESERVED. No part of this book may be reproduced or transmitted in any form by any means, electronic or mechanical, including photocopying and recording, or by any information storage and retrieval system, except as may be expressly permitted in writing from the publisher.

All names, logos, and symbols that appear in this book are trademarks of their individual organizations and institutions and have been reproduced with permission. This notice is for the protection of trademark rights only, and in no way represents the approval or disapproval of the text of this book by those organizations or institutions.

Requests for permission should be addressed to: Ascend Books, LLC, Attn: Rights and Permissions Department, 12710 Pflumm Road, Suite 200, Olathe, KS. 66062

10 9 8 7 6 5 4 3 2 1

ISBN: print book 978-0-9893095-8-5
ISBN: e-book 978-0-9893095-9-2

Library of Congress Cataloging-in-Publications Data Available Upon Request
Publisher: Bob Snodgrass
Editor: Katie Hoffman
Publication Coordinator: Christine Drummond
Sales and Marketing: Lenny Cohen and Dylan Tucker
Dust Jacket and Book Design: Rob Peters

All photos courtesy of the Brenner family unless otherwise indicated.

Unless otherwise indicated, all Scripture quotations are taken from the Holy Bible, New Living Translation, copyright © 1996, 2004, 2007, 2013 by Tyndale House Foundation. Used by permission of Tyndale House Publishers, Inc., Carol Stream, Illinois 60188. All rights reserved.

Every reasonable attempt has been made to determine the ownership of copyright. Please notify the publisher of any erroneous credits or omissions, and corrections will be made to subsequent editions/future printings. The goal of Ascend Books is to publish quality works. With that goal in mind, we are proud to offer this book to our readers. Please note however, that the story, the experiences and the words are those of the authors alone.

Printed in the United States of America

www.ascendbooks.com

Table of Contents

Dedication   9

The World Needs More People Like Bob Brenner
    Foreword by Transformation Specialist, Chris Powell   11

Tackling the C.L.I.F.   13

PART I: Growing Up   17
    C.ommitment to Excellence   19
    L.ove of the Game   33
    Athletic I.ntegrity   49
    F.aith in the Future   57
    C.L.I.F. Notes   69

PART II: Growing Me   77
    C.ommitment to the Job   79
    L.ove Lost and Found   93
    I.ntegrity Off-Duty   107
    F.aith in the Force   121
    Kelly's Perspective   145
    C.L.I.F. Notes   149

PART III: Transformation — Growing My World   159
    Transformation: What They Said   161
    C.ommitment to Good   167

Transformation: Sweet!   187
Being L.oved   191
Kelly's Letter   199
Transformation: Sweat!   203
I.ntegrity in Everything   207
Transformation: Strength!   215
F.aith in God   217
Transformation: Stretch!   223
C.L.I.F. Notes   227
Applying the C.L.I.F.   233

Get Extreme: Tips to Transform YOUR Life!   239

Unstoppable Transformation:
     Dropping the Fail from Your C.L.I.F.   257

Acknowledgements   261

Bibliography   265

About the Authors   267

Dedication

For me, and foremost, I want to dedicate this project to a God who transformed my life and who loved me at all stages of my life. This book is a testament to Him. It is also dedicated to my parents who raised me in a tough but loving environment. They shaped me into the man I am today, and I'm so thankful for that. Ultimately, though, I am blessed to have the most incredible wife in the world, who stood with me through times when I was selfish, demanding, and unloving. Kelly has stayed with me through the good and the bad and has shown me love that I didn't deserve. This book is for those whom I love most.

~BOB BRENNER

I have been blessed beyond words to be the collaborator for Bob's story and to help tell God's story as it plays out through Bob. I've prayed over each written word in the hopes that it moves people to hope of their own. There is nothing like faith to be an agent of deeprooted, genuine, whole-soul change, and because it is my desire that this book will encourage just that, I dedicate it to God.

~REJI LABERJE

The World Needs More People Like Bob Brenner

Foreword by Transformation Specialist, Chris Powell

I will never forget meeting Bob for the first time. As I addressed the group of 35 possible candidates for the journey of transformation, talking about the true secrets—the foundation—of transformation, he sat just to my left at the front of the group. He looked so uncomfortable sitting there, like an overinflated balloon, too large for the chair and shifting every couple of seconds to try to ease the pain of his weight. However, as I began to share the intricate details of the journey, he stopped moving altogether and began to absorb every word I was saying. Even though I was talking to each and every person in the room, I couldn't help but catch

Chris Powell is the trainer and transformation specialist on ABC's Extreme Weight Loss.

Photo courtesy of Rob Sims Studios

him nodding out of the corner of my eye with each and every word I said.

Ultimately, only 15 or so individuals are chosen for the journey since we simply don't have the time or resources for any more. So many people try desperately to sell their "readiness" to me during this time. It can be difficult to decipher who is truly ready and who is not.

As I spoke openly and honestly about the journey of transformation, it was clear to me that the secrets I was sharing resonated with him. A few times, I even caught him trying to hold back a chuckle or two as his new perspective on transformation "clicked," and he realized how simple and powerful it really is.

When I looked into his eyes, I could see the hope. He was ready to grow, not physically, but spiritually. He smiled back with his eyes, with gratitude and appreciation. I thought to myself, "He gets it. He's going to be unstoppable." And he was.

While it was such a privilege having a front row seat to Bob's incredible spiritual and physical transformation, the best part of the whole experience (for me) has been the amazing lifelong friend I made along the way. We had some awesome adventures over his year-long journey, and I'm looking forward to the adventures we have ahead!

Bob, I love you buddy. Keep sharing your powerful message and changing lives. This world needs more people like you.

Tackling the C.L.I.F.

"In this world, you will have trouble."

That was what Lead Pastor, Ben Davis, said in the sermon message I heard him give at RiverGlen Christian Church in Waukesha, Wisconsin, on May 20, 2012. It was just before I began my year-long, whole-body, physical transformation on the nationally televised reality show *Extreme Weight Loss*. Ben was about to talk to us, to me it seemed (as it always did seem when I had sat in the seats of RiverGlen during the last three-and-a-half years), about adversity. I knew I had a lot of that ahead of me, so I really tuned in.

The world was about to be introduced to a "me" that even I didn't like to know. In a year, I realized that *Extreme Weight Loss* would air the dramatic, music-montaged trailer for my finale episode to a huge (in more ways than one) Season 3 of the show with transformation specialists Chris and Heidi Powell. The smooth voiceover would proclaim how I was a coach who couldn't keep up with the physical demands of my police work and may not be around much longer for my wife and children. They would show footage of how I couldn't manage simple daily tasks like putting on my own shoes, climbing into my own car, or even protecting my own body against the thugs I was pulling off the streets with a bulletproof vest—they didn't make one in my size. I would stand in front of a mirror, forced to self-consciously take in my swollen image, all 448 pounds of it. It was a weight that could only be measured on a commercial scale … as if there were nothing humiliating about that. I would barely choke back tears of hopelessness and wonder at how I could manage so many aspects of my life—coaching, being a police officer, church volunteer, family man, friend—but this one thing I JUST COULDN'T CONTROL … my *morbid* obesity.

The inside of the man the world would meet had already been profoundly changed. My body, though, was still the canvas painted with years of drinking to the point of cursing out my loved ones before passing out beside them (and leaving the mess for them to clean up). Alcoholism and food addiction gave me bad skin, red eyes, suffering joints, and rolls of fat. Selfishness had punched holes through the fabric of my relationships. Shame, guilt, and embarrassment were drawn on my tired—no, EXHAUSTED face. I had lived a life on the offensive lines of football games and the frontlines of drug crimes, but I didn't have a playbook when it came to this opponent.

Morbid wasn't just a word to me.

It was my reality.

Near death.

That's how I looked.

That's how I felt.

I had gained hundreds of pounds and completely lost myself.

That's the man I would have to overcome in front of a national audience. They would see the real me. They would see my emotional pain, my failures with the family I loved, and my struggle, almost as enormous as I was, as I tried to gain back my life's purpose by losing the weight I'd gained over that lifetime.

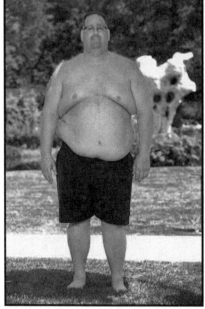

In May 2012, I was at my 448-pound worst. My health had started to fail, I couldn't do my job as a police detective effectively, and I had to give up my passion of coaching football. It was time for a change!

Was I ready? Did I want the world to know the very guy I was kicking out of my existence? And what if I failed? What if I couldn't get rid of that guy?

But that wasn't an option.

As I sat in church, I was reminded of this truth when I tuned back into my pastor. Ben was quoting Jesus. Jesus didn't tell us we *might* have trouble or we *could* have trouble. He told us that we *will*. Happiness doesn't come from avoiding burdens, Ben preached. It comes from learning how to deal with them.

The book that we were going through in our church, *The How of Happiness* by Sonja Lyubomirsky, was not a Christian book, but the chapter that discussed managing adversity in life began with the words:

> *We can rejoice, too, when we run into problems and trials, for we know that they help us develop endurance, and endurance develops strength of character.*

As I listened, I knew that this verse was what would provide me with my strength. This was what my year was going to be about. Character. Perseverance. It would be about something else, too. This was the year I would choose to live with, and lead by, Commitment, Love, Integrity, and Faith: the C.L.I.F... and a worthy climb, at that.

I'd come a long way in just a few years. There was a day when sitting in church on a Sunday morning was just about the last thing on my mind, much less in my heart. Even my soon-to-be friend, transformation specialist, Chris Powell, would later tell me he thought football was my religion (before getting to know me). For a long time, I guess it was. I had surrendered to it throughout my life. It taught me the concept of brotherhood that I would carry with me to all of the other "teams" I would serve in my life.

Growing up, from the time I could do so, I was running on the field. Then, in my adult coaching years, I was running the plays. Even as a police officer, I was running an operation or an investigation. All that time, I was also running from the responsibility to my health and my relationships. As for God, I was just plain running away.

But something changed.

It began with running back to God. That was the real transformation. That transformation is what stopped me from running away from all of my problems ... running away from myself.

It was time to stop running ... it was bad for my bum knees anyway. It was time that I start climbing toward my goals and toward my purpose. God wasn't done with me yet. The transformation that millions of viewers saw was the one on the outside, but once the soul has changed, the body is the easy part.

There's more to the quotation that Ms. Lyubomersky used in her book. She was quoting Romans 5:3–5 and the full Bible verse reads:

> We can rejoice, too, when we run into problems and trials, for we know that they help us develop endurance, and endurance develops strength of character, and character strengthens our confident hope of salvation. And this hope will not lead to disappointment. For we know how dearly God loves us because he has given us the Holy Spirit to fill our hearts with his love. (New Living Translation)

I told Pastor Ben after service that day that Romans 5:3–5 would be my sustenance in the next year. Those words would help me be extreme when I wanted to hide and unstoppable when I wanted to quit.

I wrote the verse down on a postcard and taped it to the mirror in my bathroom to look at every morning when I was in Los Angeles for the early days of taping the show. I shared that passage with other cast members of my *Extreme Weight Loss* season, and they were very thankful for it. They would share struggles, and I would answer by texting them: Romans 5:3–5.

That verse is what outlines the journey for all of us. For me specifically, it was a journey to stop running and start climbing. In fact, I had to redefine the climb completely. That's the story I want to tell you ... the story of how I went from tackling practice dummies to tackling the C.L.I.F. and how you can do the same.

PART I
Growing Up

We can rejoice, too ...

C.ommitment to Excellence

Don't you realize that in a race everyone runs, but only one person gets the prize? So run to win! All athletes are disciplined in their training. They do it to win a prize that will fade away, but we do it for an eternal prize. So I run with purpose in every step. I am not just shadowboxing. I discipline my body like an athlete, training it to do what it should. Otherwise, I fear that after preaching to others I myself might be disqualified.

~1 Corinthians 9:24–27 (NLT)

We were in awe of him.

We were afraid of him.

We gave him 100% because that's what he demanded and what he commanded.

I was in the fifth grade when a man named John Hanson showed up in our tiny town of Paddock Lake, Wisconsin, and began a youth football league. I'm not sure what brought this long-retired University of Wisconsin safety and former semi-pro player back to Wisconsin. To be honest, I never asked him until later in life and then his answer was simple—he thought we needed a team.

There was never a chance to ask as a fifth grader because practices and games weren't about chatting. They were about two things: 1) Work hard and 2) WIN. I'm not sure he'd be around for long in most of today's leagues. Just have fun? Not an option. As the great Lou Holz put it, "I won't accept anything less than the best a player's capable of doing, and he has the right to expect the best that I can do for him and the team." I can picture those same words coming from Hanson. Well, maybe he would have added a few unrepeatables in there, too.

What John brought with him to Paddock Lake was a love of football and enough financial backing from his printing company that he was able to create the Westosha (west of Kenosha, Wisconsin) Raiders. He showed up in town with a hot red Ferrari, the best training and practice equipment money could buy, and his own irrefutable coaching style. I mean it. Nobody dared refute the coach. I think he charged us all of ten bucks to belong to the league—imagine that today!

John Hanson was a big, tough, hard-nosed guy. Even his eyes were tough, drilling out from under his dark brown hair. He drove every practice and game with hot-headed, whole-hearted intensity. He cussed. He threw things. He'd never even heard of a water break and ... *he taught me how to play the game.*

Hanson was the first coach to ever affect me, so I responded to him then ... and I respect him today.

If you don't know what tiny rural and suburban towns of Wisconsin were like in the late 1970s, you may not appreciate what I'm about to tell you about my team. Hanson brought up a handful of players from Zion, Illinois, who were all black. To be truthful, these players were the first black people I had ever seen in my entire life. In a way, that was great because we didn't have any preconceptions to get caught up in the racism of the post-Civil Rights era. They were just a group of football players to help complete our team. It worked for us!

A few of us Podunk, Wisconsin kids joined these big, strong guys, these great athletes, and we became good friends and a genuine force to be reckoned with. On the Raiders team, it wasn't about who was north of Chicago and who was just plain north; it was about who the best players were to make the best team.

And we *were* the best. In four full seasons, we lost a total of just two games!

Hanson even took our team on the road. Usually, our parents would carpool us to other Midwestern cities, but one time, I remember Coach even rented us buses for this game at Scott's Air Force Base in Southern Illinois near St. Louis. We actually stayed in the homes of our opponents before game day. It was a real bonding experience but not one that took away our will to beat them on the field.

Game-by-game, town-by-town, season-by-season, we picked off the competition. We had to. Losing was unacceptable and practice to prevent it was not optional. Excellence—believe (read as: "bust butt") and achieve.

Coach drove home the literal winning point more than once in foul-languaged, full-bodied, full-colored form during practices. First, there was the time one of our linemen was pushing a spring-loaded tackle dummy repeatedly without moving it successfully. Again and again, he weakly moved the dummy inches while, again and again, Coach Hanson cursed and shouted that he wasn't doing it right. Frustrated beyond words, Coach ultimately threw down his clipboard, grabbed the child's helmet and then slammed it—crooked, tight, and with a chin strap barely able to be snapped—onto his own noggin.

It would have been funny to see that six-foot-tall, 240-pound, former safety squished into my teammate's head protection if it weren't for how fiercely he then plowed into the tackle dummy. Repeat. Repeat. *"THAT'S* how you tackle!"

Mom, watching us practice once, thought it looked like he was teaching us to street fight!

During another practice, Hanson (by this time a professional at modeling our youth helmets) pulled on the dome cover of another kid not making his tackle. Hanson had no problem then tackling the *boy* whose helmet he was attempting to wear. *"THAT'S* how you tackle!"

I did mention he probably wouldn't last as a coach today, right?

The point is that John Hanson did more than teach us to play. We had to be excellent for only one reason. He taught all of us—he taught ME—to *win*. No matter your age, no matter your color, no matter your past wins, a new game required a new commitment to excellence and a new win when the last second of the last quarter ticked off the clock and went into history. You'd better play your hardest until that final second, too! Winning became more than a goal; it became my identity … and my identity became my joy. It was an identity I would carry with me as I climbed toward every challenge—up every cliff—I faced in my youth.

There was no athletic accomplishment that I, Bob Brenner, didn't want to tackle, and tackling the dummies in practice was just the beginning.

....

My mom didn't mind my first competitive experiences being with a tough coach. Barb Brenner had maternal worries for our safety, of course, but she was also a real believer in playing the hand you're dealt as she had the life experiences to prove it.

Married to—and I'll say this as nicely as humanly possible—*a low-down, no-good, wife-beating cheater* who she would eventually kick out, Mom had my oldest brother, Bryan, in 1967. A year later, she was in the hospital delivering my twin older brothers, Brad and Brent … prematurely.

Brent was born weighing only three pounds, and both he and Brad spent their first days in an incubator. Mom didn't have it easy either. After a difficult labor, she realized she wouldn't have help with her recovery or with her new sons. This happened at the same time that she found out her husband was cheating. Here she was, a 20-something woman in the 1960s, with three baby boys, medical bills, and—because this was gratefully her last straw for that broken marriage—no husband.

Between 1967 and 1972, my mom had five boys. She juggled two full-time jobs and raising her children, and she did it alone for almost two years! She is an incredible woman who taught me to be tougher than the tough times.

Her parents could have helped; they had the ability and were willing. My mom didn't want their assistance though. She did it on her own. That was her way, and it hasn't changed. Looking back at how strong my mom was and is, I'm able to see a little of where my stubbornness comes from.

When Barb married my own dad, Bob, Sr., to become Mrs. Brenner, he immediately adopted my three older brothers. He was Dad from the start. Then, they grew their family even more by having me on November 23, 1970. Eventually, my mom had two other children, my younger brother, Bruce, and my lone, little sister, Becky. The six of us knew Mom to be a woman who persevered through it all and would teach us to do the same.

Mom still tells people how easy I was to raise. It's funny how she always thought I was "the good kid" early on. I remember my share of punishments, so I must have done a few things out of line. Mom was never the household leader who shouted in frustration that we should *"Wait until your dad gets home!"* If we smart-mouthed Mom, you could expect the punishment on the spot and not be the least bit surprised if it was a slap across the face. My parents weren't abusers; times were different and back talk simply wasn't allowed.

Mom ran the house as tightly as her kids in it. She was up at 4 A.M. every day with laundry going and the household activities underway. She managed the whole home while my dad worked long, hard hours to earn money for the large family and all of our activities. Well, all of our SPORTS. Somehow—and, as a parent of only two myself, I often wonder just how it was that she did it—Mom was there at all of our athletic events and school functions. She even served on the school board and, later, the village board.

"When times are tough," Mom would say, "you figure it out." And she did … with excellence. Her demand for it was no less than Coach Hanson's.

I guess maybe everybody can say that about their mothers, but I am who I am because of Barb Brenner. Between her history of abuse and a houseful of five boys before her daughter, she had no choice but to be tough as nails or at least as tough as the leather stitches of the pigskin. And today? I am a get-it-done type of person, and I know I get that from my mom. You don't wait for somebody else to tell you what to do. You just do it. That's what she taught me. Mentally, my mom is probably the toughest woman I know. Period. Hands down.

....

If my first coach taught me to be tough athletically and my mom taught me to be tougher than the tough times, well, my brothers taught me something else ... *just to be plain tough.*

Four boys within three years of each other made for a constant construction (or deconstruction shall I say) zone even before kids five and six came along ... *I wish I were joking.*

I'm pretty sure we broke doors, furniture, decorations, and—oh yeah—every window in the entire house at one point or another during my childhood ... *most from the inside.*

Between our troubles and Dad's schedule, Mom was stuck in that mess most of the time. On the rare occasions that my

My brothers and I hated that Mom made us wear the same shirt for special occasions. My sister, Becky, was just two years old when this photo was taken in a rare moment of standing still. This was just before Easter dinner with my grandparents in Stuart, Florida, in 1978.

folks could get out, they'd get a babysitter. Then, my oldest brother, Bryan, would send the sitter home... *he was in charge.*

The four of us—yes, Mom and Dad, it really was all four of us, including me—would play basketball in the house by bending a metal hanger into a hoop and hooking it on the back of a door. I'm not sure what we were thinking, but after too many ricochets caused too many glass panes to suffer the consequences, we finally had to move the games outside ... *it did no good.*

In the winter, we would run the basketball under hot water to soften it up enough for play. It was usually Brad and I playing against Bryan and Brent. The windows were safer outdoors, but once we were at the hoop in our driveway, we moved from breaking windows to breaking one another ... *then came the fight.*

I remember one game that got really heated. I'm not even sure why, but what followed is the part that actually sticks in my memory. In the middle of the action, probably laced with the cussing we had picked up from our folks or on the field, Brent suddenly punched me! Then, in response, Brad punched him! We all got separated by Mom, and that should have been the end of it ... *it wasn't.*

Later, with Mom and Dad not around, Bryan found Brad in the kitchen to confront *him* about Brent punching *me* as though Brad and Brent were the team this time and Bryan was sticking up for me. Everybody was taking sides! The fight wasn't over, and as my brothers argued about why it began in the first place, some pushing ensued. This wasn't a clean brawl that was kept to the floor of the kitchen. It wasn't even kept to the room of the kitchen. After one good shove from Bryan, Brad reciprocated AGAINST and then THROUGH the kitchen wall over our stairway ... *drywall flew.*

DRYWALL!

Then, Brad flew out of the room knowing he had just crossed the line! Bryan chased after him up the stairs, grabbed the back of Brad's shirt, and began stumbling back down the stairs, dragging Brad along while his head bumped, clunked, and drummed on each step. If you think it's hard to keep track of in a book, imagine what it was like in the room. Blood flowing; brothers fighting; drywall snowing; curses crying; Bryan crowing; punches flying ... chaos. CHAOS! Brad left a war-beaten trail in his wake ... *stains on the stairs.*

Right about then ... *in walked Mom.*

She stared down at a knocked-out, nearly unconscious, and certainly concussed son, and they went off to the hospital. It was just another unscheduled visit to Kenosha Memorial Hospital. It was a place where the nurses literally knew Mrs. Barbara Brenner by name. (One time, when I had bitten through my tongue at a wrestling practice, Mom had called the hospital to ask if that could be stitched only to hear in return, "is this the Brenners?") While they were off to the hospital ... *I was home alone.*

So, there I sat at home, wondering what to do when Dad returned to the house for the day. He was shocked to find holes in his kitchen, drywall on his stairs, and a path of blood through his house. To the untrained eye, it probably looked like a murder scene or, at a minimum, a break-in! Only in our home would a man not first think to call the police in fear for the safety of his family. Our poor neighbors had even numbed to our madness. Instead, it was up to me to fill Dad in on what happened ... *I told.*

My dad is a quiet guy most of the time, but none of us—including Dad—held back if there was fighting to be had. A lot more "Eff Yous" were exchanged than "Love Yous." Even Mom and Dad were known for their shouting matches with each other. Maybe they liked the passion of it, but that's the communication I watched growing up and would later share with my own wife. There were no secrets and no holding back in our house when somebody was angry or upset. We'd all heard more than the occasional bleep and blowup in our young, destructive years, and after that incident, I kind of expected to take the brunt of a profanity-laced explosion. Something worse happened ... *it didn't come.*

Dad turned around and left the house again, without another word. Had he finally lost it? As I sat, or rather hid, in the house, something that Becky and Bruce were more accustomed to, I heard the strangest sounds ... scratching and screeching, worse than fingernails on a chalkboard. I sure as heck wasn't about to move to see what it was. Mom and my brothers were still out, and I had no idea where Bob Brenner, Sr., had gone. But the grinding echoes continued, and I didn't know from where until, after a loud, creaky, squeaky crash ... *Dad returned.*

Hacksaw in his hand with a fallen basketball hoop in the driveway behind him, Dad promised, "You will NEVER play basketball at this house again ... " *and we didn't.*

My brothers and I were extremely competitive in everything we did. Dad finally reached a breaking point with our fighting. Cutting down our basketball hoop was his way of saying "Enough is enough!"

....

We had plenty of other activities to toughen us up over the years. With the basketball hoop down, we found new ways to get injured, like climbing thirty-foot tree trunks and crossing their rickety branches in order to jump out over the lake on beach days. I remember one time missing my friend's boat by inches when I tried to splash him as he drove by. I actually felt my hair get suctioned upward as the motor of his boat passed some millimeters above my skull. It seemed we were—I was—always on the verge of the next hospital visit.

I guess the heights I climbed to find success could never be high enough or risky enough. I didn't know how this pattern would continue until many years later. I didn't know how many times I would leap without looking or how long it would take me to learn how to make that leap *in faith*. I didn't know how many more times I would have the life nearly sucked out of me, just like that day at Paddock Lake beach. There was only the climb. Only the jump. Only the thrill of the fall.

Everything we did as a family was centered around this active life. When I hung out with my older brothers, it was through competition—from basketball in the driveway to tackle football in the yard. Commitment to one another was expressed through the games we shared. Excellence was expressed through sports. This was a brotherhood—my first of many. It was the number one thing—the number one thing to *all* of us. We were active. That's. All. We. Did. That's all we knew. We either interacted through endorphin-laced, cuss-filled sporting clashes and physical fights—and, to be perfectly honest, the sports usually ended in physical fights—or we didn't interact at all.

Better, then, to combine them. That's where football came in. At least when we wore our official jerseys, we would save the fight for the opposing teams. The injuries continued, and it was more than just to my joints that were already feeling the strain of too much weight for a young frame. And yet, I wanted more.

More hard tackles.

More starts.

More climbs toward more athletic goals.

I was committed to getting better, faster, and stronger. I was always in the weight room lifting weights and doing plyometrics or jump training. I was always filling up on seconds and then on thirds to get bigger, more formidable.

Never mind what all of this was doing to my body.

Never mind what it was doing to my soul by putting my worth in my size rather than in my significance.

Success in football was the definition of success in sports.

Success in sports was the definition of success in life.

This was my affirmation.

This was my climb.

This was where I put my *commitment to excellence.*

....

BECKY SAYS:

> *"It went to the game. Everything Bobby had when he was younger went to his sports. I didn't really like him. Growing up, he was about himself. He was arrogant. Even though he was six years older than I am, it really hurt when I'd try to talk to him about sports and he'd say something like, 'You don't know what you're talking about. Just shut up.' He was not nice to me. I don't really have any special memories of Bobby and I as kids. It's like there were these family groups: Mom and Dad, the first three brothers, and the three younger siblings. But really? Bobby separated himself from us."*

Becky Brenner was the kid sister in our house-full of boys who was dragged along to our games as the sometimes seemingly invisible person in the stands. Even though I never recognized it, it must have been hard for her to always be the odd one out with all of us. I didn't know until much later in life that she wanted to be there. She wanted to sit next to my parents. She wanted to support my brothers and me, and she wanted us to recognize it—she wanted *me* to recognize it.

In retrospect, Becky was sort of an extension of Mom being there when we played. I never thanked her for being at all my games. I never hugged her when I visited Mom in the stands even when my older brothers would. If you were to ask Becky how she felt about me, her big brother, as a little girl, she'd tell you she didn't like me very much. Actually, she might (quite fairly) be harsher than that and tell you I was a jerk.

She was a little girl. We, all of her brothers, were beating the daylights out of each other, and she had to hide. We were breaking windows, and Becky had to hide. We were at practices, and Becky was hidden in a sea of padded-up brothers. But, at the games, she came out of hiding. She came out for us ... for me. And I didn't even acknowledge her. She wouldn't be right to say I was a jerk. In reality, I was an ass. Who does that to a little kid ... to a little girl ... to MY sister? Me. I did that.

I didn't know then that when you commit to excellence, you're supposed to commit to excellence in life and not in just one aspect of life. Certainly not just sports … not just football. We are made for so much more than a single skill or talent, but I hadn't realized that yet. I didn't bring excellence to my relationships. I wasn't committed to my loved ones.

It wouldn't be until my 40th birthday that I could see my little sister for who she was: a girl who had to grow up, much like her mom, tougher than the tough times and tougher than the people around her. Mom was a good example for her, but I sure as hell wasn't, which is why I missed out on the relationship I could have had with Becky while we still shared a home as kids. Then, like my older brothers, I was gone. She still had Bruce at home, but, as for me, I never looked back. I needed to make some pretty big changes before I could ever have excellence in my relationship with my sister. Those changes wouldn't come for decades, and I'd wait through two of those decades before I ever admitted to her that I had sucked as a big brother when we were kids.

BECKY SAYS:

> "I'm not sure why Bobby was the way he was. Sure, he didn't respect me much, but I really don't think he liked himself very much either. When he got hurt, he kept his feelings to himself. He didn't show emotions. I don't know if it was the weight. Maybe he was embarrassed to connect to us. He didn't tell me. He never told me anything. He didn't even say that he loved me until he was forty years old."

I remember being at a bar in downtown Waukesha for my birthday. Most of my family, including my little sister, was there. I took my sister out to the car and told her for the first time in my life … in *her* life … that I loved her.

As a kid, I had turned to food to get bigger, to—in my limited understanding—get better at sports. In later years, it was stress eating. And family gatherings went from overflowing picnic baskets at the lake to huge spreads at family functions, complete with beer and other drinks.

The more I committed to my different life stages and roles (ignoring the overeating and drinking I was doing in those different roles), the less I committed to my relationships—the less I was committed to true excellence. My relationship with Becky represented that failure.

L.ove of
the Game

And now, dear brothers and sisters, fix your thoughts on what is true, and honorable, and right, and pure, and lovely, and admirable. Think about things that are excellent and worthy of praise.

~Philippians 4:8 (NLT)

December 23, 1972. A touchdown by the Oakland Raiders strips away most of the remaining time on the clock and even more of The Steel City's hope. The Pittsburgh Steelers are down by 1 in a 7-6 game against their rivals. 22 seconds on the clock.

So many unlucky 4s. 4th quarter. 4th down. On their own 40-yard line. A division championship, something left untasted for 40 years by the Black and Gold, hangs in the balance.

Terry Bradshaw lines 'em up.

HIKE!

Bradshaw is in immediate trouble, but he scrambles out of the pocket. Again, the line collapses around him and he's running out of time. Looking deep. Under pressure. He throws before Raiders linemen Tony Cline and Horace Jones close in on him. Instead of intended rookie, Barry Pearson, the leather stitches catch only the helmet of Raiders safety, Jack Tatum. It's all over…

BUT WAIT!

Franco Harris scoops up the ricochet and, not knowing where the ball even came from, he runs with it. He runs and runs and runs. He holds out an arm of steel against every silver-helmeted block that comes his way all the way to the end zone.

Merry Christmas, Pittsburgh!

Merry Christmas, Men of Steel!

TOUCHDOWN!

Some call it the greatest play in the history of the National Football League. Broadcaster Myron Cope called it the immaculate reception. Me? I call it football and ...

    I.

        Love.

        Football.

I saw the immaculate reception replayed many times as I grew up watching the 1970s Steelers with my dad and brothers. Dad was a Green Bay Packer Backer, but my brothers and I followed the terrible towel era by the Green and Gold's most deeply-seeded rival, the 1980s Chicago Bears. We watched Walter Payton break Jim Brown's rushing record on October 7, 1984. (He turned an ordinary, middle-of-the-game play into an ovation.) A year later, the year of the Super Bowl Shuffle, it was a snowy day fumble recovery by Wilbur Marshall that tied a bow on the Chicago Bears' NFC championship game. Great players on great teams playing great games ... *that* is what got my blood running.

Growing up in Wisconsin, I remember my gym teacher not understanding how it could be that I wasn't a Green Bay Packer fan, long before they were called Cheeseheads. My parents still cheer for the home team today. I told him I loved the Steelers. I did: Jack Hamm, "Mean" Joe Greene, Terry Bradshaw. I also loved the Bears: Singletary, Dent, McMichael, William "The Refrigerator" Perry. Above all ... I'll say it again ...

    I.

        Love.

        Football.

While I'm not typically of the Hunter S. Thompson school of philosophy, I give him kudos for saying, "Football fans share a universal language that cuts across many cultures and many personality types. A serious football fan is never alone. We are a legion, and football is often the only thing we have in common."

Maybe it's irony that I looked up to so many of these big linemen at a time when really big, limited to a handful of these great players, was what made you really good on the line. (And really big then is the average lineman size today with bigger still being the exception.)

It took a little time to move my love of football from the screen to the field. Even under Coach Hanson, I was really only an average player. I was always on the young side, a year younger than most in my own grade with my fall birthday. Maybe I didn't see any need to stand out with all of my older brothers leading the charges, the tackles, and the plays.

As time went on, though, Bryan, Brad, and Brent went on, too. They moved up to different, older leagues. It was as if being the oldest Brenner remaining on the line (since Bruce was a couple years younger than I) I suddenly had a spotlight on me, and it was my time to shine.

By the seventh grade, with my older brothers no longer a part of the team, I grew more confident. The more confident I got, the better I got. The better I got, the more I loved it. The more I loved it, the greater my confidence. I was caught in a cycle, and I loved the ride. When I was no longer the "so-so" little Brenner brother, I was able to be good on my own merits, and then I was able to move from good to great in the game I *loved*.

Enter Rob Hall.

Rob was a dominating force. He was physically big and had a lot of confidence. He was part of building my confidence, too. He was a great player, better than me, really. He was bigger than me, too, until I caught up to him as a freshman in high school. That's the year we really began to gel and become team leaders together. Rob was THE guy on the squad, and for me, he was the *original* "Buddy."

Before Rob, and with so many of my own siblings, I didn't really have to build relationships. They were just there for me. Built in. Family. Most of my friends were neighborhood kids and, of course, my brothers. This was an era when everybody was outside from after school until dark and parents flickered porch lights when the sun went down to tell you to come in. We played with whomever showed up and chose our games based on whatever equipment we were able to bring along on our bikes.

The Westosha football team was unique because it pulled from elementary schools all over the Kenosha County, Wisconsin area. Even though Rob and I went to rival elementary schools, and certainly would not have been in the same neighborhood parks, football brought us together on one field and on one team.

When he and I met in the seventh grade, our friendship was kind of built in through our playing positions. He was a new kind of brother for me. Rob played at running back and an occasional set of downs quarterbacking. Me? As a lineman, he'd be the first to tell you, "Bobby was my #1 Defender!"

Rob was a taste of everything MORE that the love of the game could mean for me in life. I had community outside of my hectic family. Essentially, my love of the game naturally moved me to a love of life and to love in some of the most important relationships I would have.

I was like a second son to Rob's parents, Carol and Bob. I would often escape to his house, away from the craziness of my own home packed with five siblings and one bathroom in our 1500 square feet. Don't get me wrong. I never felt like we were poor or anything. It wasn't about that. It's just that the house was loud. My parents always fought, never physically, but the proverbial trucker would have felt right at home. Plus, at the time, both of them smoked. My parents loved us, but to describe my upbringing as chaotic is an understatement.

It was at Rob's house that I enjoyed occasional sleepovers throughout high school and especially in the summer months. When we would sleep head to toe on his waterbed, he said he felt like he was sleeping on a mountain with me on the valley side. I guess that's after I surpassed him in size. We picked at each other. Teammates. Friends. Eventually, co-captains. And yeah, kind of like brothers, too, I guess. We were building something. And from building confidence, to building a bond, we moved on to building a path.

I remember one time when Rob and I laid stones for a patio. His folks had built a house near Kenosha in the country with the back of the house to the woods. They had a walkout basement with about a twenty-foot path that led to the garage. "Rise up! Rise up, sports fans!" his dad would call to us on summer mornings after late, too late, much too late nights of partying. After stumbling out of bed, we'd make our way downstairs for the day's work. Then, we'd pick up these heavy stone pieces (and in all different shapes and sizes) and fit them together. We had a lot of fun making the path and deciding which stones looked best where. It took a long time and a lot of work, but we puzzled together something unique, and we were proud of it.

Pride is exactly the right word for what else I was building inside myself during my high school years. I don't mean the good pride where you bring your best. I mean ego. Even though my friendship with Rob was (and is) something I treasure and value, I allowed my new confidence to grow to arrogance, and I brought Rob along on the many plays I was making *off* the field. Other athletes looked up to us but not always in a good way. Love of the game meant that I needed to fit the mold that star athletes are supposed to fit. Driving crazily (a lot), disrupting (a lot), dating (a lot), and drinking (also … a lot).

There were fights at parties over girls. There was tearing up the farmers' fields in our trucks. We were the good ole boys having a good ole time in good ole farm country. More often than not, my older brothers even helped to turn our weekend high school parties into full-on college bashes. With brothers of legal age, I had access to alcohol from a very young age. Then, there was the night that Rob and I decided we would sneak into the theater with a twelve-pack of beer, mind you, to see *Platoon*.

Rob was old enough to pull off a purchase in those pre-carding days. We went to Kenosha and were on our way to the theater when the blue and red lights began to flash behind us. Panic set in. More than likely, we were speeding, which probably would have only landed us with a warning. All we knew, though, was this:

- We were about to be pulled over.
- We were underage.
- A twelve-pack of beer was in view.

And I'm not ashamed to tell you WE WERE SCARED.

Rob and I decided on the stupid, teenaged response of taking off. We were racing down roads at crazy speeds trying to elude the police when my original Buddy had a plan. He whipped us into a used car lot, pulled into a spot, and parked as though we were part of the inventory. Then Rob cut the lights, and we both dropped down in our seats—out of sight. Our hearts were racing as we waited long enough to see if we lost them. We got lucky that time … and we got to see *Platoon*.

I wasn't as lucky the night I had the idea of having a gas station worker, my colleague at the time (though not for much longer), put a case of beer out by the store's dumpster. I paid him ahead of time and he just needed to leave it at the back of the store. I was going to come pick it up. Rob, a few other friends, and I had these big plans to go drinking. That was it. We were just drinking this case of beer. Big rebels, we were. Well, big, anyway. I picked up the beer and drove out to the cornfield, one of our drinking spots.

Photo courtesy of Rob Hall

I told everybody, "Hey guys, if we get busted, I'm going to get in a lot of trouble for being the one to get this beer from the gas station. We need to get our story straight." (By the way, did I mention that my dad was the general manager of the gas station where we got the beer?)

As top athletes and socialites in our class, Rob and I were popular guys and class leaders. With all of our partying, we didn't always lead in such good ways! This is our prom picture in 1988.

My partying friends and I all came up with a stupid story that we had gotten the beer from a guy walking down the street. Seriously? Is everybody this stupid in high school or was it just me? It was a tale for the ages. We didn't know his name. He just gave me the beer. I don't know who we thought would be gullible enough to believe this ridiculous story, but we all agreed to tell it.

We were just set with our details, and it was a good thing because, sure enough, the police showed up. The first thing they did was what all good cops do: they separated us. They spoke to us one at a time, and I was the very last kid to be questioned. They pulled me into the squad car and said, "Tell us how you got this beer."

I went into a long, detailed story. "There was a guy on the road. He was in his thirties. He had kind of longer hair. I gave him some money and he gave us the beer."

The police let me go on for a while, probably getting a kick out of the crazy details I was making up, before finally saying, "Bob, we already know the truth. Your friends told us you got the beer. We know it was you."

I told them, "They're wrong," and I tried to go into my whole story again. After all, I'd rehearsed it plenty, and it deserved to be heard. But they'd had enough.

That's when they said, "Yeah. You're under arrest," and they slapped the handcuffs on me right in front of my buddies.

All of my underage friends had been drinking, and they all *drove* from the scene while I got put in the back of the squad car! (My, how times have changed.) I was driven back to the gas station where I had gotten the beer; they needed to make sure that the beer was not stolen. I had to sit in the back of the squad car while the clerk was chewed out for selling to a minor. By some unlucky coincidence, my dad's boss, the owner, was also there that night. To make matters worse, I had just been drinking, so when they came to check on me back in the car, I had to let them know that I was about to pee myself if they didn't let me use the bathroom.

As the police officer escorted me in, I had to walk past the clerk who would be fired, one of my managers who would call my dad, and the owner of the company who didn't know what to think. That was the mother of all walks of shame. My cuffs came off to use the bathroom, and when I got back out, they didn't say anything to me … none of them. I was put back in cuffs and driven home where my dad was waiting for me. He had already been contacted.

Bob Brenner, Sr., met me on the porch. I was expecting punishment. An explosion. The belt even. Something. It was worse. He just looked at me, just like my co-workers and the police back at the gas station. Once the cops left, Dad shook his head and mumbled, no, more like growled, *"You'd better get upstairs before I flipping kill you."*

Except, he didn't say "flipping."

If I could manage to not get into any trouble for a year, my record would be expunged. Lucky for my future in law enforcement, I managed to stay clean or, at least, not get caught.

The truth was that Rob and I enjoyed beer. It was always about beer. Always about drinking. Never about the consequences of our "fun." The typical teenaged troubles—the fights, the fields, and the frat bashes—were never complete without a drink … or many. That was part of the image. Part of the game I loved. The popular athlete who was friends with everybody: other athletes, the kids who had nobody, and even the potheads. But their drug wasn't mine. My drugs were food and, with every bite, alcohol.

I was bigger, cooler, and more enjoyable to be around with every beer. That's how it seemed to me anyway. I was just fourteen when I first started drinking. I don't mean that I tasted something at a party. No. I was the one hosting the party! Today? I really don't need to drink anymore, and I've probably still had more alcohol than most people have had in their full lifetimes. Unfortunately, I made many more mistakes under the influence before I was persuaded to give up booze.

Somehow, through all of my shenanigans, my folks managed to keep a soft spot for me. When Dad and I spoke the night after I got beer from his store, he was embarrassed. For me. For himself. I admired my dad so much for how hard he worked at his jobs—real work with labor and long hours. And this was how I repaid him? It was just another game to me.

I had my heart on my sleeve as he and I talked it over the next day, and I cried because I had let him down. Nothing more really came of it ... just that "talking to." Maybe Dad could see past the image I was climbing toward with every stupid move I made. Maybe it was because Mom was the one who was the real disciplinarian in the house. Whatever it was, I was getting a clean slate. This was just one of many glimpses I would get over the years into a father's love. Dad worked so hard. He was always working. I messed up *his* work. I'd lost some of his trust and, yet, gained a fresh start.

....

It wasn't the first new start I'd gotten in the game of life. That came the year before when I was a junior in high school. I was a varsity starting lineman. Once more, I had played with my older brothers and watched them move on. They were on college teams now, and I got to be the eldest Brenner again.

I couldn't wait for the season ahead. In our third game, we were playing Milton High School, and I was on the ground as a play was finishing up in a pile of pads and players. I didn't see him coming when the Milton player jumped over the pile. He landed, helmet down, on the back of my hand.

CRUNCH!

Oh hell. Something was broken. I heard it. I felt it. I knew it. My eyes watered and every nerve screamed ... but *I* didn't.

Love the game? Stay *in* the game.

The hand crushing occurred near the beginning of the second quarter. I could do this. Shift my weight to my other arm in the lineup. Watch how I tackle. Keep the throbbing hand out of it. Don't let coach know.

Love the game? Stay *in* the game.

I played until halftime.

I thought I was so wise, but the assistant coach didn't miss a trick. He saw that I was holding my hand funny; playing differently. "What's up, Bobby?" he asked, and he pulled my hand toward him to take a look.

I continued to try and brush it off, saying, "It's nothing."

It wasn't nothing. My hand was mangled. He gave what was meant to be a gentle squeeze to check it out, and a bone popped right through the skin on the back of my hand ... one of the many broken pieces my skin was holding in.

I didn't expect that. I nearly passed out. "Okay. I'll go to the doctor," I managed.

The doctor never did give me clearance to play again that season. Believe me, I tried. It turned out to be a losing season. I'm not saying I could have made a difference, but I always wondered. I was devastated to finally have my time in the spotlight and then lose my entire junior season.

It was time for me to get over my image, over my own self-pride and pity. It was time to be a supportive team member. I turned my attention from on the field to off. I cheered from the sidelines. I was at every practice. If it was raining and crappy out, I was there. The coaches used me as a motivation—pointed me out to guys who weren't giving their all as an example of a guy who would love to be out there, able to play with them.

"He would die to be out there with you, and you're not even taking advantage of the opportunities you have!" I remember coach saying.

This was still my team. I still loved the game, but I was taught humility. I learned that I wasn't invincible. Having sports taken away made them that much more important to me. That much more precious. The raised value of the game gave me determination to do more—to do better. Coming out of that football season, I was beginning to feel like a caged animal ... just in time to wrestle.

·······················

Jeff Gorn. If ever a man was built to wrestle, it was Coach Gorn. He was 170 pounds and didn't stand over 5'6". Jeff had thinning, very short, very dark hair and a moustache that topped his olive-skinned face on top of a body that was solid muscle from legs, to chest, to arms. He was compact and completely in charge.

Gorn was the perfect balance of hard-nosed and compassionate. His hard-nosed approach showed in meets like the one against Burlington High School. We didn't do so well. We were down by eight, and before I hit the mat, he said to me, *"We need to let them know that they wrestled Central High School!"*

I was aggressive. I even head-butted the guy. I ended up on top. He was in the down position. I did a cross-face so hard—reaching across his head-protection and bringing him down—that I nearly broke his nose.

One tough match didn't make up for one rough meet though. As a team, we did not rise to the challenge though we were better than we scored. Drained and defeated, we hit the bus home, only to have to hit the mats back at school. Coach Gorn walked us through a practice for another half an hour.

"THIS is what you need to do in order to be great," he yelled at us. *"You didn't do it, and you NEED to get better!"*

Then, he showed his compassionate side.

After a week like that one, we expected to face a coach meltdown before our next meet and before every individual match for that matter. Hollywood has this way of conjuring up fearful images of froth-mouthed team leaders barking orders into the trembling, gloss-eyed faces of teen athletes. Yeah. We expected something like that.

But the week after our loss to Burlington, we had a practice none of us imagined coming (and one Hollywood would be bored to write). We each lay down on the mats, and Coach Jeff Gorn walked us through a visualization exercise. It started out very calming as he brought us to peaceful, comforting, and relaxing places like beaches. Then, he took us step by step back to school, back to a gym, back to the meets, back to the mats. He had us picture our matches, picture our pins, picture our wins. It was a different approach than any other coach I'd ever been with, and it helped me throughout my own coaching career.

You see, Jeff Gorn was full of tough love. *"Compete hard. Work hard. Commit to excellence."* That's what he told us.

It was an honor to wrestle for him. He was one of my idols because, beyond the tough love and beyond the love of the game, he also taught us to love one another. I felt it. I knew it. Don't get me wrong …

I.

Love.

Football.

... but, in football, I played for me. It was *my* climb. In wrestling, we competed for the coach. It was one of my greatest life experiences because I didn't do it for ME; it was all for somebody else. It would be years before this lesson about giving back fully settled in for me and a lifetime before I found the ultimate *coach.*

• •

I remember the match. That event in my life was the ultimate symbol of my love of the game and how the love of the game nearly blinded me to an even greater love.

Doak Bock was one of my greatest friends in high school. Even though he was a linebacker to my defensive lineman, we were pretty equal ability-wise. We were the big-guy athletes in high school. One kid even paid us once to be his bodyguards. Sean Dunn, a young guy who was building an "entourage" before the term was part of popular culture and slang. We never did much but follow him around.

For us, high school was all about the sports in which we dominated. While I had years of wearing the pads with my brothers, he had his dad, a semi-pro football coach for the Racine Gladiators. (I think they're called the Raiders today.) Doak was built like a wrestler (his real first love in sports): 5'9", 230 lbs., stocky, muscular—a heavyweight force to be reckoned with. For better or for worse, I would reckon with it eventually.

In football, Doak and I were both pulled up from the junior varsity team to the varsity team early in the season of our sophomore year. We told the coach, "We're ready!" Thing was, he was *not* ready. "We're good enough to start on varsity," we told him, but we practiced with the JV team.

He decided to start us with that team to see what we could do. Game one was against a local school, Union Grove, and Doak and I made 100% of the tackles. During game two at home, we nailed more than 90% of them.

"Okay," he gave in, "you're varsity."

We were pulled up to start for the rest of that season and the rest of our high school football career.

If Doak and I were equals on the playing field, he had a slight edge over me on the wrestling mat. By our junior year, he had the heavyweight wrestling slot. Of all the weight classes, heavyweight was the one that had the most prestige. I say he had "THE" slot because that's all there was; one guy on the team was the varsity representative. The rest of us were junior varsity, including my younger brother, Bruce. One lucky guy (me) got to be a "scratch" wrestler when the team went to tournament-style invitational meets.

If another team didn't have a wrestler to fit the heavyweight bill, I could be used to fill out the bracket. Only a team's varsity wrestler can earn varsity points in a varsity match. Different points could be earned by him for various types of pins and moves. Doak and I would meet up in an occasional match, and, if points were on the line, my shoulders would be on the mat. Most of the time, I didn't mind taking one for the team. We would even work to make sure Doak's pins would be worth the most possible points. I didn't know if I could beat him yet, and more team points for a tournament would mean more tournaments for the team. This was the right thing.

Doak took 5th place in the state championship tournament our junior year. Maybe that tournament lit the fire under me to desire it for myself. By the end of that year's season, whether it was just time on the mats or through Coach Jeff Gorn's and Doak's leadership, I got good. I got very good. Doak was my friend—one of my *best* friends, but I didn't want to take the fall anymore. I wanted THE varsity slot. I went into my senior year saying just that.

At that time in my life, I went after whatever it was that I wanted, even if it meant I was taking it from one of my closest friends.

When you wanted to move up on the wrestling team, you had to have a wrestle-off. After two years of choreographing the perfect pins, Doak and I knew each other's moves pretty well. It's not like we could fool each other or try to catch somebody by surprise. These matches were all about who was biggest, strongest, quickest, best. You tell the coach before a tournament that you want to wrestle-off. It's just how the game is played. And me? I love the game, right? This wrestle-off, though, was, by far, one of the hardest things I'd ever done. The only way that I could get the spot I wanted was to try to take it away from my friend.

I won the first wrestle-off 6-2. A wrestler can challenge again after a wrestle-off, and, out of respect for Doak's three-year varsity slot, Coach Gorn gave us another match.

In the second match, I beat Doak 8-1 and he never reclaimed the title. Coach was really gracious to us both. He pulled us aside and said, "This was really hard. That took a lot of courage."

I wonder, if I could go back to high school with the wisdom of adulthood, would I have challenged Doak? It was my opportunity. I felt I had to take it, but in my heart, I know it was hard for both of us. I know it was hard for him. He was upset. We got along really well and got through the season, but he had to cut down to a different weight class entirely, and I was the heavyweight varsity wrestler that went to the State Tournament our senior year.

I had beaten Doak for the varsity spot on the wrestling team, and going into the State Tournament, I was 29-3. My excitement and expectations were high. To then lose in the first round was devastating. It was the hardest defeat of my athletic career, and it still bothers me today.

I thought for sure I was going to win State, but then I lost. When people tell stories about back when they were in high school, they are always focused on the event … whatever that event is for them. A dance. A party. A class. A tryout. A teacher. A scrap in the hallway. A kiss in the parking lot. I was no different. It was the meet for me. What I didn't realize was that the day would be branded even decades later, not just in my memory, but in the memories of my family.

A far greater love was taking place in front of those mats than the one that was taking place on them. They were all there: Mom, Bruce, Becky, team, neighbors and friends, and, most importantly, Dad. I lost the match, but I won that day and didn't even know it. And, for the love of the game, I almost missed something else, too.

Doak Bock. I was so close with the guy. He was a good friend. He was very quiet. Not everybody got him. Nobody ever knew how he felt, but I was able to draw feelings out of him. Our senior year, I felt for him, too, because I knew that I took something away from him, and those would be the feelings I would never hear about … feelings of betrayal.

....

While I was focused on the game, I didn't pay a whole lot of attention to something else that Doak and I shared. Before every football game our senior year, we would go read the Lord's Prayer before playing and we continued the tradition in college. It was common. Often before games, the locker room was really intense, so we would prefer to go somewhere quiet. That was me, always trying to escape the chaos, just like my own home. I don't really remember how the pre-game tradition started. We read the prayer, though—

in the weight room,
on the steps,
laying out on the benches,

—wherever. We would read the Bible together, and when we finished, we would pray quietly before the game.

Doak was the one who brought his Bible and initiated it. I didn't do it on my own. Church was for Sunday—an obligation for living under Mom's roof. Doak's Bible was highlighted in yellow and underlined all over the place. He actually studied it. There's a Charles Spurgeon quotation that says,

> *The Bible that's falling apart usually belongs to a man who isn't.*

Maybe that's how he was able to support me and cheer for me when I had chosen to wrestle him. Maybe his Bible (that was falling apart) is what kept him at our pre-game ritual even after that senior high school year. Doak ended up going to Carroll College with me, but he didn't wrestle. He just played football. I don't know if he just didn't want to make the transition or if it was lost confidence.

I never asked. I'm not sure I would have liked the answer.

I lost track of Doak Bock over the years, not running into him until a 25th Central High School class reunion, but, together, we grew and shared a love of the game. More importantly—

    in the weight room,

        on the steps,

           laying out on benches,

—he shared seeds for another love. They wouldn't bloom for many years.

I still haven't told him, "Thank you."

Athletic I.ntegrity

I will refuse to look at anything vile and vulgar. I hate all who deal crookedly; I will have nothing to do with them.

~Psalm 101:3 (NLT)

I was barely pulling a 2.0 grade point average as I went into my sophomore year wrestling season. Coming in as the next Brenner brother in line, teachers considered me to be pretty good by comparison, but Brenner brothers were known for being great athletes, too. That's what got the coaches talking. Jeff Gorn was planning on keeping me around for a few more years, and these grades weren't going to do. He told me as much.

"What're you gonna do? You want to play ball? That's not gonna happen. Not if you don't get your grades up!"

I never did have one of those coaches who held punches. Gorn was no different. Coach supported me tremendously. My grades weren't the greatest, even after that conversation, but I did graduate at almost a 3.0. Most importantly, college didn't end up falling off my list before I even got to it.

An athlete's integrity should be just as intact off the field as it is on the field. That's a lesson that Gorn needed to enforce, and one that led to other decisions in my athletic career and life.

There have been studies done for years showing that we're learning a lot more than the rules of the game when we're playing a game. It's easy for me to look back as an adult and see where that was happening even if, in high school, I was really only going for the win.

I remember one win that was easily in our grasp back in my Westosha team days. We were playing in Milwaukee. This was Hanson's team, so we only knew how to play to win, but this game was something more than that. We didn't just want one in the W-column, we wanted *ANNIHILATION*.

The score was 35-0 and we were still going strong; we had a lot left. The other team was defeated on the scoreboard, they were defeated in their body language, and they were defeated in their hearts. I'll be the first to admit that we were reveling in the victory to come. Everybody was going crazy for what was going to be one of our hardest whoopings ever.

As we got on in the game, our defense was in (which was miraculous in itself). Coach Hanson called us over. "Let 'em score, guys," he told us.

We must have looked like we misunderstood, so he said it again. "It's 35 to nothing in the 4th quarter. LET. THEM. SCORE."

Loud and clear.

Even our parents were wondering what he was doing after that play, but he wasn't done.

After they scored, Coach called over our kick returner. "As soon as you get the ball, you're going to fall," he told him. "You're not going to score."

Again, Hanson was loud and clear.

That day, at that game, we won. We beat the pants off them. BUT …

What we didn't do was embarrass them. We showed *them* mercy, and Coach John Hanson showed *us* athletic integrity. I loved my coaches far more than my accolades.

•••••••••••••••••••••••••••

Even though I had the honor of working with so many talented coaches over the years, I was always just a good player on great teams. That changed during my senior year of high school. *I* changed. My senior year was my "coming out" year of athletics; I got real recognition. All of my climbing ... all of my gaining ... it was paying off. My talent grew. My confidence grew. And, if I'm being honest, my body grew and my arrogance grew. I felt that "unstoppable" feeling for the first time in my life.

In addition to the wrestling varsity slot, I excelled on the football field. I was a first team all-conference offensive *and* defensive player. I played everything except for special teams—kickoff, kick return, and punt return. I was in all of the local news, and I was even scouted by a handful of colleges. Northern Illinois University sought me out. The Universities of Michigan and Minnesota knocked. The University of Wisconsin, Madison, home of Bucky the Badger, took notice, too. The thing was, I was not the prototypical lineman at 6'0, teetering on 6'1", and 250 pounds. Most linemen are 6'4" or 6'5". You need those big wingspans to block big bodies and high passes. As big as I was, I wasn't big enough. If I could have eaten to gain height, I probably would have.

I wonder if that idea stuck in my head for longer than I realized.

For all the initial interest in me by that first convoy of major universities, I was passed over. I wasn't going to be on the team unless I would choose to do a walk-on tryout. I didn't see a *Rudy* movie happening for me though. I didn't make the attempt. My parents weren't really involved in the process either. They left the choice up to me.

I wanted to go to the University of Wisconsin, Whitewater. I remember the pride of being recruited pretty hard by them; I even signed a letter of intent. The decision was made. I was going to go.

Then, in the spring of my senior year, my high school held some sort of elimination tournament for our baseball team. I was feeling so excited and even a little proud when I saw the man in the UW-Whitewater purple colors about to walk near me.

It was head coach Bob Brezowicz of the University of Wisconsin, Whitewater football team. He had come to the baseball game at my school and probably would even say hello to *me*. I had been visiting the Whitewater campus just two weeks earlier when the coach had told me how excited he was for UW-

Whitewater, for the football team ... and for *me* being a part of all of it. I was sure this would be another of those coaches who helped to grow me, just like Hanson, Gorn, my high school football coaches ... all of them. This relationship with the Whitewater coach was my next step because we had made such a strong connection during my UW school and team visit.

As Coach Brezowicz approached me, I was feeling like the big man on campus, and I grinned when I called to him, "Hey coach, how you doing?"

He said nothing.

He looked at me.

We locked eyes.

He ignored me.

He saw who I was and then ... he just *ignored* me!

I got it. The message was perfectly clear. This was a new world. What he had given me was a sales pitch, and I later told him as much. In my generation, there was a saying that told us to beware of the person who is nice to his date but mean to the waiter. It was the kind of thing Mom might have said to Becky. At UW-Whitewater, I was the date, but that day in the bleachers, I became the waitstaff.

At that time, my brother, Brad, had committed to go to Carroll College (now called Carroll University) in Waukesha, Wisconsin. Brad was transferring from UW-La Crosse in western Wisconsin. I had met one of the Carroll football coaches, too. Coach Herrick from the college had been at our last football game earlier in the school year, and he spoke to me in our locker room after we played. I had been getting letters from the local area school ever since then.

After the incident at the baseball game, I called Brad and told him "I want to come to Carroll."

"Let me talk to Coach Masonholder," he said. (That pretty much translated as: "We're getting the band back together!")

I got a call later that same day, and Coach Masonholder said, with *genuine* excitement, "We would love to have you come to Carroll."

Coach Masonholder told me to get my application in and I would surely be accepted. Make no mistake. It was my athleticism, not my academic prowess, that got me in. Thanks to Coach Gorn, though, my academics didn't keep me out. (And thanks to a few pushes from Coach Masonholder throughout my college years, I kept the grades up enough at Carroll to stay in their program, too!)

As for Coach Masonholder, it may have been a surprise gift for him to invite me to Carroll's football team so late in the college entry game, but he gave me the gift of this new team, a new brotherhood, and, eventually, the rest of my family. I was meant to start my college career on *this* team led by a man of true athletic integrity.

....

Another one of my coaches in my Carroll days was Sparky Adams. Sparky coached for thirty years. This wasn't a coach I worked under; rather, I worked beside him. At this point in his career, he wasn't even being paid. He worked for free! He had a son at Carroll (David, who today coaches one of the top high school teams in the state of Wisconsin in Mukwonago), and Sparky just loved the opportunity to work with his boy and the other college players on his son's team.

Carrying a fair-skinned, stocky body on his 5'9" frame and in his 60s when I knew him, Adams epitomized the picture of what an old football coach should be.

> *Merriam Webster—COACH: (noun) A person who teaches or trains an athlete. See: Sparky Adams.*

Sparky pulled a grungy hat down over a head full of gray hair just to the top of his thick glasses. He was usually drinking a Dr. Pepper on the sidelines when he coached, and he sported a pocketful of hard candies to hand out as though he were everybody's good-natured granddad.

The nicest guy in the world, Sparky Adams could talk football for hours non-stop … everything about football. He would talk a lot about the plays, the positions, the players, and the past teams. The old. The new. The field. The sidelines. The good. The bad. The ugly. Sparky just plain loved the game of football, and he was happy to bend the ears of people who would listen to him tell them as much.

Sparky Adams was put with me by the Carroll College staff when I was made the offensive linemen's coach in 1994. I had to coach the same guys who, a year ago, I had lined up with to play the game! I used my own learning as a player and applied it to my coaching. These are also the same guys I used to go out partying with, drinking to late hours of the night, or—more realistically—early hours of the morning.

How was I supposed to tell the guys, *"Hey! Don't go out drinking Tuesday night or it will ruin your Wednesday practice!"*

I hadn't led this team by example in years past. Sometimes, I could get away with a lot more because I was lucky. Maybe it was because of my athletic gifts. More likely, though, it was just a greater tolerance for too much alcohol and not enough sleep that gave me the ability to have late, irresponsible nights and still follow them up with great practices and games. I had already garnered respect from the team as a player because they had seen me play and they had seen me practice. They had appreciated my performance on the field. I didn't translate this to the sidelines though. Looking back, I wasn't a very good coach, which I think was one of the most difficult things for me.

That experience of coaching offensive linemen in 1994 would be my first, and so I looked back to the model of my own very first coach, John Hanson. Just like Hanson, I yelled and screamed and cussed. The only thing missing was an undersized helmet jammed onto my head. This was what I did, my own version of a hard-nosed approach to coaching for a couple of years. Then, they teamed Sparky Adams with me … intentionally.

I was this twenty-four-, twenty-five-year-old guy. I pretty much thought I had all the answers and couldn't imagine what this old codger could teach me. I decided I would just put up with him. After all, by 1994, I had been a part of the program for five years. I was a pretty decorated football player. Sparky was an old guy and an outsider. It was pride and arrogance that kept me from wanting to learn from him.

We were in the third week of practice, and the team was working on inside runs. The purpose of an inside run was for us to work on our blocking skills to create holes that assisted the run game. The defensive line would practice stopping the run. The starting left guard would pull right, trapping the inside tackle, and the running back would cut inside. It was a quick, inside trap.

During the practice, I stopped the guys constantly. I was a coach now. It was my job to instruct. Instruct I did; I barked out black and white orders in colorful language.

It was one of those times when Sparky called me over with a "Hey, Bob, can I talk?"

He was perfectly polite about it at first, quietly pulling me aside. "Sure," I said.

Then, I'll never forget when the hard-candy-toting Sparky Adams used my language to get through to me. "Pardon my language," he said, "but you need to shut the flip up!"

(Except, like my Dad after the dumpster beer incident, he didn't say "flip".)

"You need to get more reps in," he said. "They run. You stop. They run. You explain. They run. You talk. They're not even listening anymore, Bob. You need to flow your practice. You can still instruct, but these guys are only going to learn by doing, and you are getting in your own way."

"Whatever!" That's what I said, but the truth was I knew that he was right.

Sparky was onto something, and my own pride was getting in my way again as much as my non-stop all-stops. I didn't want to hear what he had to say. Even so, from that day forward, I changed. Eventually, I started to seek out old Sparky Adams. I asked him questions. I sought his advice. Some of his approaches were old school, but a lot of his concepts were right on.

Because of Sparky's advice, for the first time in my life, I started to get out of my own way. I would end up coaching football for another sixteen years before I finally left the sidelines. Five of those years were at Carroll College. More importantly, eleven of those years were with my son, Jordan. I can't imagine ever having coached Jordan with my old approaches of calling out and cussing. Sports mirror life. All of the principles you learn, including excellence, dedication, winning and losing well, and working as a team toward an objective, are life lessons. I coached those principles at the high school level. I wanted them to learn football, but I also wanted them to learn how to apply football's lessons to life. That was the bigger takeaway than the actual game. When I was coaching at Carroll, I only taught them about the game. I was an immature twenty-something-year-old kid, and I wanted them to play how it was supposed to be played … how I played. It wasn't until later that I learned there was more to football than football.

I had a long way to go to get out of my own prideful way in other life areas, but Coach Adams lit the spark to the possibility of a life full of more than athletic integrity. He gave me a glimpse of a life full of self-integrity.

F.aith in the Future

I know that you can do anything, and no one can stop you.

~Job 42:2 (NLT)

The years before my Carroll College coaching were filled with my Carroll College clashes on the field. After I made the decision that I wanted to play for Coach Masonholder, instead of the University of Wisconsin, Whitewater, a lot of big, talented dominoes fell into place on what would become my line. There were six of us from my high school team there at Carroll, including my friend Doak. My brothers Brad and Bryan were waiting up there for me, too. We all got to play together.

The first meeting we had, I'll never forget. There were about a hundred of us in the auditorium at the school. I was probably one of the biggest guys at 270 pounds at my same height of a little better than 6' tall. At the start of the meeting, all of the coaching staff was introduced. Then, they called for all incoming freshmen who were only 17 years old to come get a waiver to play. When I stood up to get my waiver, everybody turned around and looked. They couldn't believe I was only 17. I was already feeling like the new big man on campus.

As a large guy, I remember when they faced me opposite Ricky Cooper in our first full-contact practice. He was 6'3",

270 lbs … and the best guy on the team! I remember he had a beard, which made him look as though he was about 30 years old. I remember thinking, *"I'm just a kid! They put me opposite a MAN!"* When the play started, I lunged forward and Ricky just slapped me aside like a rag doll. That was my introduction.

The locker room after that first practice was full of smack talk. Offensive players were giving a hard time to the defensive players. Defensive players were threatening the offensive players. This was all new to me. I had played both sides of the line before. I just didn't understand how they didn't like one another. And they were serious! These guys were out for blood!

The talk between the two lines was filled with expletive-laced threats of, "Wait until we get on pads."

And then? We *did* get on pads.

The tensions were high between the offense and defense—I was actually scared. When we finally hit the field together, we played just ten plays … and it was THE MOST INTENSE ten plays I'd ever played in my life. Every tackle turned into a pile.

"WELCOME TO COLLEGE, KID!"

It was the first time in my life I ever remember being afraid to play the game of football, but it was exciting. It was electric. My adrenaline was pumping. Even my eyes had trouble settling down in their sockets … and I knew IMMEDIATELY I was right where I was supposed to be.

Ironic that Ray Kroc, the founder of McDonald's, can best sum up how I felt in that moment: "The two most important requirements for major success are first, being in the right place at the right time, and second, doing something about it."

This became the weekly norm. I played against and with these older, bearded guys. Alfonso Morales was from Bradley Tech, Milwaukee. He had also started as a freshman, and I blocked for him. He was a great running back, but offensively, our whole team had a ton of talent. The line had a 270-pound per person average. They were big. My own high school's center, Jim Barnett, joined us at Carroll. Craig King "Kong" was 6'6" and our biggest guy at tight end. Besides our size, we just really gelled as a unit. Dave Dorn led us at starting quarterback.

He had been out the year before because of an injury, and he came back ready to win. He was a little cocky—a regular Jim McMahon. Dave called his own plays. The thing was, he would win with them, so the coaches didn't mind.

I came into my own that year, all over again.

I remember our third game that year, against Millikin University. It was a tight game, and only a couple of minutes were left in the fourth quarter. We were on the 30-yard line.

Al Morales was our running back, and we were running a play called the *29 Bounce*. I would downblock the defensive lineman covering the pulling guard. He would also block down to the linebacker. The pulling guard would pull left to trap or kick out the defensive end. This would open up the field for an outside run.

Let me tell you, Morales was five feet eight inches of solid muscles with pigeon toes and bowlegs. Even at that size, he was laterally the fastest running back I have ever seen in person. My job was to downblock on the defensive tackle; my teammate had to pull left to open up the track for the running back. I kept destroying my block, but the play had gotten stuffed a couple of times.

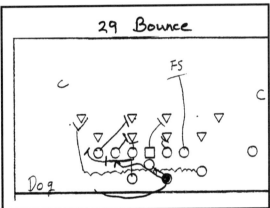

This play was called the 29 Bounce. It was one of my two favorite plays as an offensive lineman. We scored many touchdowns off this play.

I was ticked when my offensive line coach, Jim Weisman, pulled me aside. I was furious. The other guy kept missing *his* tackle.

"I am blocking the hell out of my guy, Coach! I just want the guard to block the defensive end so that we can score!"

"Bob," he calmed me down. "You gotta control those things that you can control and all that other stuff? Don't worry about it. Do what *you're* supposed to do and let me worry about the rest."

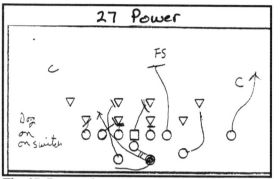

The 27 Power play was my second favorite play from our 1988 Carroll football playbook.

Weisman did take it upon himself to worry about the rest. Instead of the 29 bounce, he called a 27 power. It's just what it sounds like. All power. All in your face. Get the ball. Get it quick. Cross the goal-line. It was really something to watch Morales, in all of his bow-leggedness, running through the hole and sweeping into the end zone to score!

I gained confidence after that game. I no longer felt like the nervous kid, and I used Jim Weisman's advice throughout my coaching career. Really, I've used it throughout my life.

Then, there was Dick Lange. He was the linebackers' coach, and his linebackers could do no wrong. They were the best on the field at all times. He was also put in charge of the punt team. As a freshman, I remember they would try out different combinations of people to see who could make that special team operation work best for the team. Even though I was weighing in at upwards of 270 pounds, I could still move pretty quickly, so I auditioned for the punt team. I ended up as a starting lineman, so they decided it wasn't the best place for me. They wanted to get me off the field to be with the rest of the offensive line. No punt team for me.

One practice, I remember running down on a play, and I always hustled my tail off in practices. I wasn't necessarily a sprinter, but when I was doing drills, I would move fast. I ran down the field quickly and made a tackle.

"Brenner, come here!" Coach Lange called out to me.

I ran over to him and he said, "I gotta tell you something. If I had a first round draft pick to be on my punt team, you'd be my #1 pick, Baby!"

It was the first time that a coach had really singled me out to say something like that. Here I was, just a freshman, and he made me realize the power of positive words and belief in abilities. He gave me faith in myself.

....

I know my mom, after all the time spent in church, thought we'd turn to religion for faith. The time would come, but it was about football at this stage in my life.

Mom used to take all six of us kids, loaded up into the station wagon, and drag us by force, not by choice, to Salem United Methodist Church. Barb Brenner was adamant about our attendance. We never talked about God or prayed at home. We weren't raised with "Christ in your heart." Church wasn't an act of worship or pursuit of a relationship; it was an act of tradition and the pursuit of obligations. Every Sunday, Mom took us; Dad would join us on Christmas and Easter (a Chreaster.) In the fifth grade, we began youth classes; in eighth grade, we were confirmed; and, when we graduated, we no longer had to go ... so I didn't go.

I did go to every football practice though, and I did go to every football game. And some of that Bible teaching must have sunk in because I remember that guys around me were using steroids; I had access to them, but I never took them. I felt that God had gifted me with natural talent and size, and I didn't want to tarnish that. So, I did have some supernatural faith in place, but mostly it was faith in football.

Coach Masonholder made me part of a brotherhood; I learned about life through Sparky Adams; I gained confidence and control through Jim Weisman; and Coach Lange would soon leave me the most important part of my adulthood. I had faith in football because it gave me faith in the future. I had lost out on some of those major colleges who had once looked at me, but I gained an extended family. The patriarch was Coach Masonholder. I also had great uncle-like mentors, such as Sparky Adams, and great advice from people like Jim Weisman. And what about Coach Lange? He had an incredible daughter named Kelly. She would very soon become Kelly Brenner: MY #1 draft pick, my smokin' hot wife, the mother of my two children, my partner in Christ ... and the undeserved, undeniable, unconditional love of my life.

••••••••••••••••••••••

Kelly would have to wait awhile before we became more than acquaintances. In the meantime, I was still building the relationships that, for many years, would be my priority: my friendships. My guy friends, my teammates, my pals, my buddies always came before even my greatest love.

The first time I met Mike Schultz, he was a freshman at Carroll College and I was an upperclassman. Schultz was the picture of a football stud. He was six feet, 180 pounds of lean muscle. What stood out to me, though, was his confidence. He had a level of certainty not many young guys bring to the table. He was borderline cocky, to be honest, but in a fun way. It wasn't distracting or off-putting.

We were a veteran offensive line at this point, so it had to be a little intimidating when Mike became our starting quarterback just four games into his freshman season. Still, when he came into the huddle, he was in control. Any leadership doubts disappeared because that's just a good quality you don't always get to see in a quarterback. I was really impressed with how he handled himself and liked him right away. He wasn't the best quarterback I'd ever played with, but he was one of the toughest and definitely one of the best leaders, too.

Later, Mike told me that he actually had been scared to death of me, this big, aggressive, good player. Fooled me. That's part of the game, I guess, and he knew how to lead the game … even if he did have to learn how to handle a loss. When we played Beloit College later during his freshman season, we ran the ball well but had a few fumbles. Mike threw a few interceptions, including one within the opponent's five-yard line … just as we were about to score. We lost. He felt responsible.

"Heads up, Schultz. We win as a team. We lose as a team," I told him. (Thanks, Coach Jim Weisman.)

Mike said that those words meant a lot to him because another player had told him he'd lost the game for us. Past playing together, we coached together and became great friends through that experience.

Mike hugged me when we would greet each other or say

goodbye, which was new to me. He was outwardly expressive with all of his feelings, and that was rare for men in general. At least, it was rare among the men I'd known in my life. Mike also taught me loyalty. ANYTIME I needed him for ANYTHING, he was ALWAYS there for me. He helped me with everything in my life. Whenever trials and tribulations took place among his friends, he'd pick up everything and go. I remember him driving down to Indiana in the middle of the night for a funeral to support a friend. Mike Schultz was the consummate Buddy I wanted to emulate.

Maybe I did a little too much of that "buddy" time, but there were other things I got from him that changed how I would communicate with people and set me on a path of truthful expression that I could tap into years later.

It took me aback the first time he did it. Mike and I talked on the phone all the time. One time, before hanging up, he said, "Love ya, Buddy!"

I remember looking at the phone as I hung up kind of like, *"Yeah. Okay. Weird."*

But he didn't do it just once. Every time we spoke, it ended with "Love ya, Buddy." It stopped seeming weird after awhile, and then it started feeling normal, and then I started to expect it. I know Mike lost his dad when he was only 11 years old. Maybe that made him appreciate the people he cared about and the time we have together, and he knew it was important to express that. That's just my speculation. I never asked, but Mike was kind of the first guy who, by his example, showed that it was okay to say those words to other men.

Besides Mike, the first guy I decided to try it on was probably Rob Hall. I'm sure he felt like me when I'd first heard the expression. *"Really dude? We're guys. We don't say this unless we're drunk."*

Like me, though, my friends have come around. Even Chris Powell, who I first met at the start of my physical transformation, has been known to toss me an occasional, "Love ya, Buddy."

As the final part of my television episode was filmed, I had to walk from the limousine to the football field. The first person I saw was Mike Schultz. He told me that he had no idea where

I'd be coming from, and he was actually trying to stay in the background. He didn't know that I was going to walk right past him. He was right there. It had been about nine months, and quite a few pounds, since he'd seen me. I got the hug, of course.

"Love ya, Buddy."

....

Love doesn't always come conveniently. When we were still in high school, long before we met the women who would one day hear our marriage vows, Rob Hall and I made a vow to each other. We promised that we would be the best men for each other at our future weddings. Rob had the opportunity to play his role much sooner than anybody expected. I had a bit of a "shotgun wedding," as it's called.

After high school, though, Rob had gone down to Florida for a new beginning. Golf had taken the place of football for him, and I was sort of that anchor to the hometown. He said that it was always so good to " ... have Bobby for him back home." I was the one main friend from high school that he stayed in contact with in order to keep that hometown perspective as his surroundings and climate changed.

Rob had gotten hurt in his senior year of basketball, and his dad had assumed that Rob would just go down to Miami on the golf scholarship, serve his time, so to speak, and then return home to take over the family business. Nobody assumed he'd fall in love with the lifestyle, the weather, and, yes, the golf, of Florida. (Not to mention, he would meet his own future wife, Heather, down there, while at college!) He did fall in love with Southern Florida, much to the shock of his dad, and he's lived there ever since, far away from the Wisconsin weather.

I still saw my buddy at the holidays. When he visited me in college, Rob and I would go drinking and then hot tubbing off campus. We were still the leaders of the party, even states apart from each other. We would visit his folks and reminisce about the crazy stuff we did in high school. We would leave his poor parents in shock over all of the completely irresponsible crap we got away with. They really didn't have a clue about those years. It's a wonder they continued to treat me like one of their own.

I hope Carol was able to laugh about it before she passed away in February 2012. I know she would have been one of my biggest cheerleaders if she had lived long enough to see my *Extreme Weight Loss* transformation, but at least she and Bob Hall saw my faith transformation, long before I attended her funeral with my Buddy, Rob.

With Rob already visiting at Christmas and in the summer months for bouts of 9-hole beer golf, Brewer game beer buses, and other beer-related college partying, it would have been okay for him not to come home for my wedding. That's a lot of travel for a guy who had to fly home.

When Kelly and I decided to get married, though, Rob came up to fulfill his duty. He was kind of shocked about the whole thing because it all happened so fast, but he was a great best man and even seemed to take pride in it.

Kelly and I got married at Salem United Methodist Church, and my parents' backyard took the place of a reception hall. The ceremony was small, and the food was simple. I was young and jobless, and my bride had our baby, our future daughter, Kayla, on the way.

When it was time for Rob's wedding to come around, he didn't even think about a best man. He knew me and just assumed I'd be there. He never asked, "Hey, Buddy. Because of your change in circumstances, are you going to be able to come down?"

It was sort of late in the game when I realized Rob would simply *expect* his best man to be there. Maybe I held off on telling him because, deep down, I knew this about him … about us. The wedding was getting close, and I had to explain to him that I just couldn't make it down. Money was tight. I had a second baby on the way at that point. I thought, maybe if I could just make something happen in the next week, I could go. I asked for that week to get back to him.

Nothing changed and, as sorry as I was, I just couldn't do it. I couldn't make it down to Florida. Right up until the ceremony, he thought things would change, but I wasn't able to be there for *my* best man as *his* best man. He was so mad that I broke our pact.

Partly because of our different lives at the time and partly because Rob felt really shunned by my absence at his wedding, we parted ways. It wasn't a falling out so much as we just moved forward in our lives without each other. We had a little contact; we exchanged cards, dropped a hello through family from time to time, and the like, but we didn't share anything substantive for about ten years. He had been my friend since my Westosha Raiders days, all the way through high school and in college, but, all of a sudden, we were like mere acquaintances. Rob became "a guy I knew growing up," something I never expected him to be.

Moving on with Rob was his new wife, Heather. Heather has cystic fibrosis. Most of her life, her case has been very minor compared to others with the disease. She was hospitalized for the first time at age 19, but her lungs weren't bad enough that she qualified for a transplant. Today, she has cystic fibrosis-related diabetes and has even contracted cancers from all of the medications required to treat her illness.

Rob will tell you that Heather gets one hundred percent of the credit for mending our friendship. Life for everybody is hard. Period. Nobody was promised this world would be easy. (In this life, you will have trouble, remember?) And relationships are the hardest part of all. Add the constant stress of disease to a relationship, and without the right support, you can run yourself into the ground. Rob needed a friend.

When he spoke to his wife about the fact that he didn't have anyone he was really close with, somebody he could talk to about "real" things, he told her that only one person had ever been that to him. It was me. She began working on him for days, then weeks, then months, to reach out to me and, finally, he did.

We both apologized for the wedding, for our stubbornness, and for letting so much time go by. It had been ten *years* since we had spoken, I mean *really* spoken. Only ten *minutes* into the conversation, we picked up right where we had left off. I had my buddy back. Only six months after that initial phone call, we saw each other. We introduced our families, and we've been great friends ever since.

Looking back, our relationship was like that flagstone path we had built for his parents' patio all those years earlier. Some of the pieces of our lives were crooked and uneven. (I was certainly a little misshapen for a very long time.) Few of the stones went together the way you'd expect. Rob and I both had to lay the work out, and we both had to make our own design. It took a long time and a lot of work, but in the end, we had puzzled together something unique and we were proud of it. I'm still proud of, and grateful for, our friendship, which, like that patchwork, flagstone, patio path was and is a foundation. We still celebrate on this foundation today. And we celebrate *with* our wives. Heather and Rob have been married for twenty years.

My faith in the future was even better with faith in a past friendship. If I could help give him a little faith in the future too, that's one foundation stone I was happy to lay. I can't imagine climbing life's climbs—life's cliff—without Rob Hall, and I'm glad I don't have to.

C.L.I.F. Notes

I was an athlete in high school—not a scholar athlete, just an athlete. After Jeff Gorn got on my back to get my grades up, I would take whatever tools I had available to make the grade. Today, the internet makes all manner of information available at your fingertips for free. When I was in high school, though, our only quick information came in the form of CliffsNotes. Covering everybody from Shakespeare to Charles Dickens, the little yellow and black pamphlets (if you could manage to get a hold of them at the library) boiled down books like *A Tale of Two Cities* to a tale of two chapters, give or take a few pages. CliffsNotes would cover those types of questions you knew your teachers would ask and even break them down for you into categories like *theme, literary device* (such as symbolism), *style and language,* and *character insight.*

I can't say that life has ever offered me a CliffsNotes version of my own daily events, but I have discovered my own notes from living on the C.L.I.F.... . my metaphor for climbing toward life's achievements. I look back at the chapters of my life and see the *themes* that were central to it, the blatant *symbolism* that was always present, the *lifestyle* I was choosing, and *insights* into my own *character.* These are the C.L.I.F. Notes I have decided to remember, to reflect on, and to redeem in my life.

Theme: Believing in Me

Growing up, I don't have that story about a dad who beat me or verbally abused me, and I was blessed to have a mom who wouldn't put up with that kind of thing. At my worst, she still considered me a teddy bear, maybe with a few stitches here and there. So, I don't have a hard-luck tale for you. We were never rich, but we always had enough to fill our bellies, so I don't have a story of poverty either. I think our society today likes to tell the rags-to-riches stories, and I have a lot of respect for the people who come from difficult situations and make a great life despite that fact. Who doesn't love a great comeback game, right?

I'm not actually able to relate to the troubled kid-done-good story. Instead, I understand the tales of people who were blind to the blessings they did have. I understand people who abused those blessings, ignored them, took them for granted, or misunderstood them. That was me. That was me before my transformation. Truthfully, I was always surrounded by people who loved me, provided for me, and believed in me. I had coaches, my mom and dad, my sister and brothers, Doak, Rob, and eventually Kelly. I had friends around me all the time, no matter what role I was in at those times in my life.

Living in the moment, I felt that all of those people believed in me because of sports. In wrestling, they believed I would win State. In football, they believed I would get a scholarship, and they believed I would be a Division 1 football player. They believed I might even go pro! (In my dad's case, I think he was being overly optimistic by believing I'd be a Green Bay Packer lineman one day.) Even strangers believed in me when they saw me play.

People always say to recognize what you have. I had it all. Except I didn't know it. I discovered later in life that you should look at why you have it. I had all of these people in my life who believed in ... ME. They didn't believe in just my ability to make it in sports. They believed in who I was and wanted me to be better at being him.

I was so committed to getting better, getting faster, and getting stronger—primarily in football—that I didn't see how committed so many people in my life were to me just being happy ... fulfilled. I needed to learn, and wouldn't for many years, to make a commitment to the relationships I had with others. They were the people who believed in me and in the person I could be beyond just the athlete.

Lessons in Commitment:
- **Take stock of the relationships you have.**
- **Take stock of why you have those relationships.**
- **Believe in the person you are, rather than the things you do.**
- **Commit to excellence in those relationships.**

When it comes to commitment, the real C.L.I.F. Note lesson was to also commit to the person that all of the people in my life already believed in. I needed to commit to myself because I could be something great with or without the sports. All of those who believed in me realized it, but it would take me awhile to learn it. Instead of pouring myself into the people around me, I dragged them around in my entourage, much like Sean Dunn had asked of Doak and me. I needed to commit to real relationships.

Commitment meant to prioritize sports.
I misunderstood what priority was all about.
I needed to learn to put people first.

Symbolism: Climbing with Me

None of us know what's on the other side of the cliffs we face in life. The climb, the cliff, is kind of a game we play with ourselves. And, really, I treated my own climb like a video game of sorts. The character I chose was a football player, and, along the climb, I would pick up all the bits of gear I would need.

Football players are big. So, I needed to grab some fast food. In fact, I needed to collect every fast food token I passed! Football players are cool, so I needed to be the guy who got the beer. How much can I carry? How much can I hold? Football players are popular. My character needed to stop along the way to give time to every teammate, to every "buddy." Parents and sisters were just part of the scenery. I didn't need to waste time in the places that wouldn't get me to the top. That was the goal. Keep climbing. Get. To. The. Top.

The problem with video game-style climbing, or with my *love of the game*, is that I never looked up and never looked back. I was only concentrating on the few pixels before me.

Besides my sister, I would have seen my kid brother, Bruce, just beneath me, climbing to catch up. Funny I should think of him now since he's also the one I used to play Pac Man with for hours on end. I dragged him along on all my crazy escapades, too.

I was always going up and never taking note of who was following my lead. Bruce had even repeated my dumpster beer crusade. (Although he never got caught, so apparently he made some improvements to the plan.) The thing was, Bruce was watching. He was always watching me. Besides not knowing what was ahead of me, at the top of my climb, I didn't know what was behind me, climbing with me.

Lessons in Love:
- **See who's looking up to you.**
- **Choose to be a character worthy of imitating.**

When it comes to love, the real C.L.I.F. Note lesson was to be an example of love to those who looked up to me. I was always so busy climbing toward a goal that I didn't notice the people hanging on the end of my rope. When things got really ugly before my transformation, those were the same people who anchored me and pulled me back.

> *Love meant to love my team.*
> *I misunderstood brotherhood in my own family as a "real" brother.*
> *I needed to learn to express love to my family.*

Lifestyle: Mounting the C.L.I.F.

I really did feel like I was on top of the world when I was growing up. I was doing all of the things that, to me, were the perfect image of a perfect football player in a perfect life. If I am honest with myself, though, I was also an imperfect brother, holding up an imperfect image in an imperfect reality.

I was trying to be a picture. I wanted to be the big linemen on the professional football teams. I didn't even know them! I saw them physically. I saw them athletically. I would catch them in the thirty-second clips of post-game coverage. As winners, they were everybody's friends. As losers, they might let profanity slip when they thought the camera wasn't on them.

That's exactly who I became.

I never knew the personal stories of the big football players I had looked up to. I just saw who they were on the field and in those candid camera moments. I should have taken the time to discover who they were in life. That would have been truth. William Perry fighting weight, Terry Bradshaw not keeping his marriage together, Joe Namath going down a destructive path of alcoholism. I always saw the indulgences, never the demons of the players in the game I loved. If I was honest with myself, there were greater things toward which to strive.

Lessons in Integrity:
- **Be honest with yourself.**
- **Strive to be more than an image.**

When it comes to integrity, the real C.L.I.F. Note lesson was to discover the true meaning of integrity. My integrity wasn't in place off the field, drinking too much, putting fun before family and hunger before health. I needed to find something much greater toward which to strive. I needed something more than the perfect picture. I needed a perfect Creator; that day was still a whole chapter of my life away.

> *Integrity meant keeping the game clean.*
> *I misunderstood integrity off the field.*
> *I needed to learn integrity in other areas of my life.*

Character Insight: About Growing Up

I believed in the principles of faith after all of those weekends at Salem United Methodist with my family. The people in the church were good and my mom was and is an amazing woman who managed to get us all to the services weekly despite our chaotic family schedules. Like a lot of people, though, I wasn't actually driven by those principles talked about in a language that felt ancient to me. The Bible was dated, and I was full of youth.

One of the most important principles they taught in church—although I didn't really understand it until my studies years later—was that God will provide. If I had believed that, I wouldn't have been busting my tail so hard to be a person who, like I said before, was not a real person at all so much as an idealized image of happiness and perfection.

I may have had faith in the future that I would have, but it wasn't because of anything I learned from my religion. It was because of my work. Of course, I ignored all the bad works I had done. I didn't consider the partying, the underage drinking, the cussing, and the general selfishness that I portrayed in my life. The bottom line was that I was going to be somebody because I climbed.

Lessons in Faith:
- **Let go.**
- **Accept that you can only be yourself.**
- **Trust that you have a purpose.**

When it comes to faith, the real C.L.I.F. Note lesson was to just be my best me, not an ideal image, and to believe that that person has a purpose. My faith in the future was really just faith in myself, and that isn't real faith at all. Real faith is trusting what you do *not* control.

Because when it came to control … I was about to lose it.

> *Faith meant that I controlled my own destiny.*
> *I misunderstood the meaning of faith entirely.*
> *I needed a faith that went beyond my own abilities.*

Extreme and Unstoppable
What They Meant When Growing Up

The dictionary defines *Extreme* as: "of the character or kind farthest removed from the ordinary or average." *Unstoppable,* in that same dictionary, is an adjective to describe that something "cannot be stopped or surpassed; unbeatable." On paper, those words sound like worthy goals. Who wouldn't want to be extraordinary and unbeatable? The problem is that, just as with Commitment, Love, Integrity, and Faith, I needed to find ways that were mentally, emotionally, physically, and spiritually healthy to which I could apply extremes and unstoppability.

When growing up, I was *unstoppable* in sports. I was a four-season player (football, basketball, wrestling, and baseball), and, between those seasons, I continued in sports with my brothers. I guess, retrospectively, it was a good thing, because while growing up, my *extreme* was eating. My quantity of intake was extreme. My fat intake was extreme. My salt intake was extreme. My sugar intake was extreme. These things all added up to an extreme caloric intake.

It was a different time. Nutrition was not taught in schools, and my mom's generation was of the "clean your plate club" era. White bread was cheap. White pasta was cheap. Peanut butter and jelly were cheap. Sugary cereals were cheap. How else do you feed five boys, plus another three people? In addition, our meals were of the traditional American set up with a hunk of meat, a white potato, and a vegetable taking a backseat rather than the front row it should have. Nobody ever said you were eating too much.

Nutrition, like God, was really not expressed in our house, and I think that was a common approach at the time. Considering my eating habits, I'm grateful for what was unstoppable in me. If not for sports, the extremes of my eating would have led to obesity much sooner. The longer weight is a problem, the harder it is to get under control. I was gaining weight, without any understanding of how to be truly healthy.

The number of articles in the world that address the importance of nutrition for athletes is growing every day. Unfortunately, it's difficult to know what's right because there's so much disagreement out there. Simple searches on the internet for these topics will pull up tens of millions of advertisements, articles, answers and other pieces of information and, chances are, they aren't all good suggestions. I can guarantee, though, that non-stop athletic strain and a steady diet of fast foods and sugars is the wrong way to go. (Although I'm sure you could find a few links in that search listing of tens of millions that would attempt to suggest otherwise.)

The trainer I worked with during my *Extreme Weight Loss* transformation (and still today) shared an image on his gym's website. It was a picture of an iceberg with the words "30% fitness" written on the piece of ice above the water and "70% nutrition" written on the huge remainder below the water. This is a man who owns and runs a gym. Even he recognizes that you aren't going to get healthy through exercise alone. It just. won't. happen.

As Ann Wigmore (of the *Ann Wigmore National Health Institute*) puts it, "The food you eat can either be the safest and most powerful form of medicine or the slowest form of poison."

I had begun poisoning myself from a very young age, and then I beat myself up on the field, beat myself up on the mat, beat myself up on the court, and beat myself up on the diamond. Unstoppable and extreme, or rather, *extremist*, is who I became. Poison and torture are the weapons of extremists, but I was doing it to myself. I was a terrorist against my own physiology.

The damage I was doing to my body was nearly as huge as I was. My joints were a mess with unnecessary stress caused by the excess weight. My muscles never had the proper foods to recover and build, so I negated a good deal of the working out. My heart was working overtime, constantly having to be raised to and then past a target heart rate while under the strain of what I was doing to my blood vessels. Not to mention, my heart was managing this workload with the added difficulty level of too many pounds of weight. Eventually, those internal messes I was making were bound to show up on the outside.

I was extreme, and I was unstoppable. I was also on the path to a heart that *would* stop at an extremely early age if I didn't find a better way to apply those words. I needed to gain something besides pounds and lose the habits that were putting me on a path of self-destruction.

It was time to grow up.

PART II
Growing Me

*We can rejoice, too, when we run into problems and
trials, for we know that they help us develop endurance,
and endurance will develop strength of character …*

C.ommitment
to the Job

But those who won't care for their relatives, especially those in their own household, have denied the true faith.

~1 Timothy 5:8a (NLT)

I got into a great college because of family and football. Some of that family even thought my life was going to be in football. Dad, in particular, dreamed about me wearing his green and gold colors one day. Sure, that may have been farfetched, but Dad influenced me in other ways, too.

When we were younger, Dad was a water patrol officer. Then, he served Paddock Lake until their police department was swallowed up by the local sheriff's department. I always saw Dad working hard, serving his community in order to serve his family. He wasn't there for all the games, matches, and picnics, like Mom, but he took care of us in the way I thought men should. He worked often, hard, and long, to put a roof over our heads and feed the appetites of a houseful of athletic boys, including those from Mom's first marriage, who were equally his own sons, and my sister.

Dad was exhausted. He was often in physical pain. Once, he was on medications for his back, which led to an addiction that had to be overcome. (I guess addiction ran in my blood, too.) But every day, he got up, went to work, busted his tail, and brought home the bacon. (Of course, in our house, it was often literally bacon!) How could I grow up around that and not learn from the dedication that he had to supporting his family?

It wasn't just because Dad had been in law enforcement that I considered it for myself. I loved football, but that actually became the vessel to my college education where I was able to become a cop. Even early on, when I was a kid, this was a goal I had. In the third grade, I had a teacher named Miss Fox. She had us write a paper about what we wanted to do when we grew up. I said I wanted to be a police officer. I got an "F" on that paper (back when teachers were still allowed to give an "F" to a student).

Mom held on to the third-grade writing though. Years later, she ran into the teacher and told her, "By the way, my Bobby is a cop today."

I can't imagine Miss Fox really remembered one student's goal paper all those years later, much less what grade she gave it. But leave it to Mom to stick up for her Teddy Bear!

As much as my family was a part of my career choice, football prepared me for law enforcement, too. Besides being a pretty formidable size, I had spent the majority of my childhood in a brotherhood. First, I was a real brother with five other siblings. Then, from the time I was a Westosha Raider, until I was making tackles for the Carroll College Pioneers, I was on a team. That's what teams really are—brotherhoods. I was used to that sort of buddy relationship, which was just as much a part of blue-collar service jobs as it was around the wrestling mats and on the football fields. I could be a team player even when the team wasn't in sports, and I always wanted to be the team player on a winning team. What better place than on a police force? It was still a brotherhood … just a different uniform.

So many of the classes I had to take for my bachelor's in Criminal Justice had nothing at all to do with being a cop. I guess that's the case with a lot of majors. Sociology proposed views that weren't my own and taught them as fact. Economics was just something I really didn't relate to; it wasn't something I could identify with. But the class on evidence? That was the class that convinced me that this was the field for me. Steve Centenario, who is a retired deputy district attorney for Waukesha County today, taught the evidence class, and I found the class incredibly relevant. This wasn't a social work class. It was from the prosecutor's perspective, and it was filled with information I could relate to actual police investigations. Criminal Justice, investigations, and detective work—that was where I really wanted to work.

Life put me on the fast track with school, and with family, so I also hopped on the fast track when it came to my police career.

- Spring 1991: finished one more semester of school in order to meet the requirements of my major in Criminal Justice
- Fall 1991–Spring 1992: took time off school
- Got married
- Fall 1992: went back to school (really just to play football because I had two years of eligibility left on the team)
- December 1992: got a job at the Waukesha County Jail
- February 1993: had my daughter
- Fall 1993: went back to school again, now a married father
- 1994: started coaching at Carroll College, continued working at Waukesha County Jail

I had twenty-four credits to go before getting my full degree, but I was married with a kid. My wife was making minimum wage. I was attempting full-time school, a full-time job, and overtime work just to be able to buy groceries and pay the bills. I was a senior, but I couldn't do it all anymore! I decided it was time to jump into my career with both feet.

From college football player, to full-time working family man; from the college campus to the county lockup. It was all a transition I never really had the opportunity to appreciate. This was my new life. This was my new commitment. It was just like Dad's commitment for all those years—commitment to the job, commitment to financially take care of my family, commitment to provide for a kid … when I still felt like a kid myself.

....

I had been working at the Waukesha County Jail for one week when I learned just how ugly and dirty the job of correctional officer could be. We had a difficult prisoner who had to go to court. It was our job to escort a defendant from a cell to the courtroom. This guy decided that he wouldn't have to go if we couldn't bring him. That idiot literally covered himself from head to stinking toe in his own feces. Tip to all the kids out there who make a dumb mistake that lands them in a cell; covering yourself in crap doesn't get you out of court. It just makes you look like (and smell like) crap *in* court, and that won't help your case.

We had to put on hazmat suits to go in and get the prisoner, slipping on the brown mess he'd left us. He became wild to the point that we were forced to subdue him with a taser and catch his sloppy body. There was human crap all over the place! How did he even have that much in him? We cuffed his wrists, squishing right over the layer of excrement he had applied, and threw on his shackles. We managed to wipe him down while he was still feeling the effects of the taser, all the while wanting to puke away the putrid nastiness; but we didn't need to add vomit to the bodily excretions. We got him to his feet and ready to go, a labor that left us all covered in his fecal matter. He was still crap-coated from head to toe, minus the areas we were able to slop off of him, when we were able to escort him to the courtroom, still in our hazmat suits, looking like we were dealing with patient zero and smelling like we'd been taking an afternoon dip in the city sewer pipes.

We walked right into the courtroom in this crazy getup … we in our suits and he in all his pungent glory. After an admonishment from the judge, you can imagine he was no happier to go back to the cell than he had been to leave it in the first place. It took a lot of strength to get him into a restraint chair in his cell, and I learned for the first time that strength and size would be just as important in this career field as on the football field.

My size kept growing, and it was good to be big.

Within six months, in part because of incidents like the hazmat prisoner, which required a guy with a strong constitution and a strong body, I was chosen as the training officer for incoming officers.

I often worked third shift, and my size and strength were very helpful at that time of day. We would get in a lot of people who were drunk or combative, and they needed a guy who could handle them. Sometimes, my weight alone would even serve as a deterrent.

My size kept growing, and it was good to be big.

Another part of the job was cell extraction. If a criminal was in a group cell and causing trouble, we would go in after him to put him somewhere else. We used these big, blue blocking shields, held them in front of ourselves and rushed into the cell to pin a guy in the corner or against a wall. It brought me back to my blocking drill days because I always led the way in to stop these guys. Once they were pinned, other jailers would come to both sides of the prisoner to restrain his hands and feet while I held him.

My size kept growing, and it was good to be big.

There were even times when my size meant the difference between life and death. It's public record that David Stokes was a dangerous man. He shot his neighbor. He shot one of our deputies. Stokes was a pretty violent dude, so we had him on twenty-four hour watch. By that, I mean WE. WATCHED. HIM. Eyes on him every second. Staring contests with an empty-eyed man. His case was very high profile, so we weren't going to let him get away with anything, and we were pretty sure he had worse things in mind than requiring us to wear hazmat suits.

I was on duty the night a female correctional officer passed him his tray of food. Stokes managed to grab her clipboard from her. This wasn't about taunting the correctional officer. David Stokes had grabbed himself a knife.

Even before we could get in the cell, Stokes had torn off the sharp-edged, metal clip portion from the board. David began to slit himself, smiling at me while he did so ... the sadist. It was gushing and graphic; this was going nowhere good, and it was going there fast. We got the cell open and rushed him. Stokes had just been slitting his own exposed skin, but once we got in the cell, what was a tool for cutting himself became a weapon for stabbing. In the chaos, we couldn't even assess who might be hurt.

It was a mess.

Blood was everywhere. (Let this be another lesson to kids. You never know what various substances have been on those cell floors. Maybe it's best to just avoid getting into them at all.)

We managed to pin the violent man down and grab his slashing arm. I needed to get the metal out of his hand without getting stabbed in the process. I slammed his hand against the wall and the piece dropped.

We were alive. Stokes was subdued.

My size kept growing and, on that night, it was good to be big.

I remember when I was brand new with the Waukesha Sheriff's Department. I was working third shift, and it was probably around midnight. I still didn't have a clue what the job was about when a woman called 911 and screamed in total panic, *"There's a man in my house, and he's going to kill me!"* Then, the phone was put down, or cut off. I don't know. But that's all we heard.

That was it!

We didn't have anything else to go on!

I got called up to go with a team out to the address. We mobilized very quickly, but I didn't know how any of this worked yet. I assumed I'd be one of the guys guarding the perimeter of the house while the SWAT team interacted with the gunman.

When we got to the home, it turned out to be kind of an old farmhouse—like something out of the Waltons. I couldn't imagine violence erupting in this picture-perfect country scene. The crickets were literally chirping, the air was fresh and cool, and here I was being ordered into a stack. It didn't seem right.

The stack is a line of men "stacked up" to go into a door. A stack is used when you're going into just one single-doored entrance because you won't fit two by two or you don't have the ability to scatter into several entrances. In football terms, receivers were on the perimeter of the farmhouse. Offensive linemen were in the stack. The quarterback was the guy who would break down the door.

We had an offensive play that night. Our objective wasn't to score a touchdown; it was to save a life. I was able to apply my football experience to this career experience. You'd think I'd be relieved that I was a lineman, just as I'd trained to be for my whole life, but I wasn't. I really wanted to be a receiver that night ... on the perimeter. Shoot. I wanted to be on the sidelines, and what the stack is NOT ... is the perimeter and certainly not the sidelines. I knew this was what I'd trained for but to move from a position where the bad guys are behind steel bars to one where it's your job to get them there frays the nerves the first time around.

I swallowed hard.

I was going to be in the thick of the mess. My adrenaline was pumping. My brain was swimming. I was cussing in my head. My heart was racing. It was like the chaos in my house growing up when I used to run away to Rob's place. It was like the chaos in the locker room before a big game, and I would run off with Doak. But I wasn't home, this wasn't a game, and I couldn't run. I felt sick. I was in this stack with SWAT guys who had ten or more years of experience, and they made ME the number two man! Green as the farm grass ME! There was the man who would break down the door and then ... did you hear? ME! *'Holy God,'* I was thinking ... it wasn't a prayer so much as a curse, but it wouldn't hurt if He heard me.

Because it was dark out, and the curtains of the home were a sheer white, we could see into the kitchen, and lucky for us, the people inside couldn't see out. Maybe I just told myself that for the oh-so-needed shot of courage. The gunman was shaking his gun, active and engaged, in police lingo. We could hear him screaming, *"I am gonna kill you!"* so we had to move fast ... so fast that we didn't realize he had already shot the door's lock to get into the home.

That was a game changer. It meant that when the SWAT team

leader pushed in the door, he wouldn't be running into a solid force. The door would break apart at the locking mechanism, rather than be forced open in a more controlled way. We made our hard, fast entrance, and the stack lead got carried with the momentum of the broken door as it flew in, taking him to the ground. He was out of offensive position. Sacked.

DAMN IT!

Time was racing, but somehow my brain seemed to have time to play it all in slow motion.

Flying in the door, all of a sudden, I became the first face the gunman would see. I was in front of him, looking him in the eye, with my gun pulled, and my hand on the frame of my Glock.

"DROP THE GUN! DROP THE GUN!" I was yelling. I don't know where my voice even came from. I was sure there were tears of fear—panic gasps just behind it. *"You canNOT let your team down,"* I thought.

Mom in my head, *"Be tougher than the tough times!"*

Coach Hanson in my ear, *"That's how you do it!"*

Coach Gorn in my memory, *"This is what you need to do to be the best!"*

Coach Jim Weisman in my heart, *"Control what you can control!"*

But all that mattered was the training in my hands.

Sparky Adams in my mind, *"Get out of your own way!"*

"Calm down," I told myself.

Despite the swarm inside of me, my eyes were focused, my hands were steady. I was moving my finger from the frame to the trigger guard. I was pointing at him, focused on him, watching him, and trying to figure out his next move. This was going downhill fast.

He was pointing his gun at the woman now!

Chaos!

I was gonna have to kill this son of a bitch. Holy God, I would have to murder. *Are You up there?* This must be what they mean by no atheists in foxholes. My throat closed up. I wanted to throw-up. I was literally milliseconds from being forced to pull the trigger … when he dropped the gun.

I grabbed him. Then, the guy behind me grabbed him.

I breathed. Had I stopped breathing earlier? I was breathing now, right? I paused to actually feel the air enter and exit my lungs. The team was in motion, setting up for the next play.

It was over—except for my still speeding heart rate.

Coach Lange's voice cut through the noise, *"You'd be my #1 draft pick, Baby!"*

When we searched the gunman's vehicle, we found a murder-suicide note. That day we saved TWO lives—a man who needed help and a woman who would have been dead without ours. That day …

It was good to be big.

At my biggest, I wouldn't even have fit through that door, but as I was getting started in law enforcement, big was part of the intimidation I needed. Size was an ally against criminals like David Stokes, the farmhouse gunman, the men who needed to be subdued, disarmed, cleaned up, and taken in, and the inner fears that needed to be quelled to do the job.

This was what I did. I gained a new understanding of the importance of my work. Keeping it was necessary to prevent losing lives. This was my new commitment … commitment to the job. I gave it my all to support my family, and I gave it my all because, thanks to the criminals I faced, I had to, ready or not. Even Albert Einstein recognized the need for total commitment to a job when he said, "Only one who devotes himself to a cause with his whole strength and soul can be a true master. For this reason, mastery demands all of a person." Pretty soon, I would give all of myself to police work and it wouldn't leave room for the things … the people … that mattered most.

....

"Where did we get it?" My brother Bruce and I asked ourselves this question all the time.

The crazy hours we *worked*, the way our thoughts were occupied with that *work*, the long-term goals for our *work*, the need to be in charge at *work* … it was always WORK with the two of us.

"Where does that come from," we'd ponder in conversations on the phone?

But, ask my sister, or my mom, or my wife, and you'll know that we two brothers just couldn't make the obvious connection—we got this work ethic (this work addiction?) from Dad.

It's weird that we could wonder why we kind of turned out the same way. Bruce works in construction, and he works very hard and long hours.

I took my imitation of Dad's approach to work a step further by tracing some of his exact steps. Bob Brenner, Sr., became a water patrol officer for Paddock Lake in 1976. He later went to the police academy and became an officer for our little Wisconsin village for eight years. He was with them right up until they became a part of the sheriff's department. If Dad could put food on the table for six kids and a wife who stayed home with them, as a cop, I could certainly do the same for (eventually) two children and a working wife.

Growing up, Mom was everything. She graded the homework, read our reports, and expected our efforts, not our perfect grades. She was not only the loving mother and the nurse but also the leader and the disciplinarian. She was at every activity and usually took us out afterward for ice cream. She took us on the picnics, usually with an overfull lunch she had put together containing as much as four sandwiches per boy. That was Mom. She did everything and, seemingly, did it all alone.

I love my dad, and I honor him, but he just wasn't there. He couldn't be. He loved us and cared for us, but he always worked. I remember wanting to go with him all the time. I'd beg him, and he'd find something for me: picking up trash, cleaning, painting, anything. I invited myself along.

Even when Dad was home, he would get sick from exhaustion, and it was usually pretty major. He had back injuries and kidney stones. My wrestling match at State, where I lost, was the first and last time he saw me wrestle. He didn't see me play football until college. We had a few fishing trips growing up, and those were great. I wouldn't say that we had huge, specific bonding moments; it was usually quiet, but it was just nice to be with him.

The truth is, growing up, there was never a time that we didn't have what we needed, and we also had a lot of what we wanted. But the big memories about getting things are really about those times when we were all together. Christmas was always big for us, probably because Dad worked so much overtime to make it come together. I remember one year when Bruce got this nice, red Magnum bike and I got a Dallas Cowboys bike. I also remember that Dad was there.

I loved my dad and he loved me, and it wasn't because we said it a lot or hugged, but just because I knew what he did to provide for the family. We didn't really talk about the work either. It was just done. Dad was about work as far as I could tell.

As a police officer later in life, I never took work home with me. I saw a lot of things on the job that were no good. Real police work is nothing like *Mayberry*. It's more like *America's Most Wanted*. I didn't bring that bad stuff back to my house and family each day. I thought that was enough … always having the ability to separate myself from my job. I knew cops who took the stress of what we did home with them. It was so detrimental to their marriages, to their families, and to their lives, so I made the decision that I wouldn't talk about work at home.

Instead, I would take my kids to the park, and we'd shoot some basketball hoops. I showed the two of them proper baseball hitting form and my son a proper football stance. I taught my kids to throw a football or we would have a catch. I connected with them doing the things that my dad couldn't be there for when I was growing up. When it came to time with my wife, Kelly, I would try not to talk about what happened at work. We would spend time together without necessarily going there.

I didn't hide my feelings after a tough day, but my whole approach to family time versus work time was actually a lot like playing ball in college. Family was that calm before the storm; it reminded me of those times laying flat on my back out on the benches with Doak. I would get centered. That's how I prepared. As an adult with a job, family centered me. Then, just like crossing the orange line into my

Carroll College stadium lit the athletic fire in me, I'd cross the threshold into the station, and I'd be ready to go as a cop. It was just like that—a light switch. When I left the football field, the game was over. When I left work, I went home. The job was over. The games do count, and they prepared me to put those principles to work in my real life.

Because I was a part of my kids' lives when I was home, I thought I was accomplishing the task of work and family balance better than my dad's generation and better than the cops I knew who had brought relationship-killing stresses home after work. The thing was, to be there for my kids and wife, I actually had to BE THERE. What I didn't change about my learned approach to work was how much time I spent doing it.

....

Kelly alone in parenting ...

"When I was pregnant with Jordan, Kayla was only 9 months old. I worked at an orthodontist's office with regular hours and Bob's shifts always rotated. I remember one of those pregnant mornings, in our little downtown, pink-roofed home, I needed Bob to watch Kayla, but he hadn't come home. I called the babysitter, and she was great about it, but I was livid, especially when he finally came stumbling up the stairs when I was on my way out.

I gave Bob the silent treatment for two weeks and even told my father-in-law that I wanted his son out! 'I won't let you do that,' his dad had said.

We never really addressed the situation. Bob would usually apologize when I gave him the silent treatment, and I'd be back to where I was, trying to keep it all together. We were young, and we had young kids. It was stress upon stress upon stress."

....

My working hours, especially when I got into the narcotics unit, were unpredictable and long. I usually didn't even check in with Kelly, particularly if I was working second or third shift.

I would think, "What does she care where I am or if I'm late when she's just at home or in bed anyway?"

See, even if I didn't share my feelings—of exhaustion, stress after a hard day, disgust with some of the people in my world, hopelessness over some of the things I witnessed as a cop and narcotics officer, and fear for the lives and well-being of good people I knew—the feelings were still there. I didn't speak nicely to my wife when I came home after those long hours. Kelly would, in turn, get frustrated with me. My dad was always so quiet, and my mom was an over-the-top extrovert who would let everybody know how she felt. I grew up with their marriage and their roles as an example. I learned from it. I didn't know that I had more than just work. As a father, I had to also work on my relationships. Instead, the stress ate at me, and it drove me to eat.

I got my dream of being a police officer, and I took a lot of pride in that work. I would one day learn how to honor that commitment to the job in a whole new way by trying to use my work field as my mission field ... not just the mission of solving a crime, but the mission of changing the heart of a criminal. Until that time, I needed to refocus my commitment to my family.

All this time, I thought I was climbing toward something great through my work and through keeping work in its place, but I was leaving my family behind. It was time to grow a new commitment.

L.ove Lost and Found

If I could speak all the languages of earth and of angels, but didn't love others, I would only be a noisy gong or a clanging cymbal. If I had the gift of prophecy, and if I understood all of God's secret plans and possessed all knowledge, and if I had such faith that I could move mountains, but didn't love others, I would be nothing. If I gave everything I have to the poor and even sacrificed my body, I could boast about it; but if I didn't love others, I would have gained nothing.

~1 Corinthians 13:1–3 (NLT)

It was August 1988. She was the resident's assistant for the dormitory, living on the second floor, and she was also dating a pledge brother in my fraternity. I was a lowly freshman on the first floor. Every night, she would do her walk-through on our floor—the men's floor—in our co-ed dormitory, and she was (and still is, might I add) a *total knockout*. More than that, she was a knockout who knew football! That was my in. I would always find an excuse to get her to stop in my room and talk for a while.

Kelly Lange.

Smart.

Hot.

Football Aficionado.

Yep. That's how I remember first meeting her, the woman I would one day marry.

Carroll College was a small community. Kelly was always around all the athletes. She was Coach Dick Lange's daughter, and she handled the statistics for football up in the press box on game days. Hot co-ed who knows football and is smart to boot. It was time to make nice with the coach's daughter! We got to know each other that way, and there was also a lot of intermingling between my fraternity and her sorority. But we never really got beyond that friendly, flirty, football-family stage until after Coach Dick Lange passed away in February 1990.

Kelly's dad and the man who called me his #1 draft pick was gone.

The team really admired Coach Lange. To all of us, he was just a good guy. He was always in really great shape: his shirt was pressed, his hair was in place, he was always shaven and tucked in, and even his socks and shoes were perfectly paired and displayed under exactly the right break in the crease of the pants. Coach Lange carried himself so well. Most of all, he loved his players.

None of us knew that Dick Lange had an enlarged heart

Coach Lange was one of the most incredible coaches we had at Carroll College. He was also Kelly's dad. He demonstrated every practice that he loved his players. After he died in 1990, Kelly and I bonded more.

although we knew he was all heart when it came to his players. All of us were at the funeral.

Kelly and I began talking more after she lost her dad. Even though Dick never knew me as a son-in-law, I'm glad he wasn't a stranger. Kelly and I bonded over him. Kelly, of course, knew a different side of the man—all of that perfect grooming meant he was a pretty strict guy in other areas of his life, too. Strictness is how he dealt with his kids, which was very different from how he handled his players. (She was from order and I was from chaos.) Regardless of our very different relationships with Dick Lange, Kelly and I both respected him, and it gave us a solid footing that was deeper than all our flirtations.

....

In November 1990, I was at a bar in downtown Waukesha, just a few blocks away from the Carroll campus. I was recovering from what would be my first ACL reconstruction of my knee, so, even though it was so close, I had driven rather than walked down. Kelly came into the bar—it was a popular hangout for those of us at the college—and she sat beside me. She had just broken up with my roommate, and she was talking to me about how she couldn't find a good guy to date. Kelly was kind of throwing it out there that, *"Hey! I'm single!"* (At least, that's the way my twenty-one-year-old ears heard the words from the smart, hot, football-loving woman in front of me.)

"I'd *love* to take you out sometime," I volleyed back. The words just kind of hung out there for the rest of our conversation because, in reality, I was already dating somebody else. Even then I was a selfish jerk.

At the end of the night, it was late and as cold as you would expect a lake and riverside Wisconsin town to be in November. For the first and last time, I was grateful for a bum knee that led to the offer I was about to make. "I have a car," I said. "Would you like me to drive you home?"

If I had gotten my act together by that point in my life, this is where I would say, *"The rest is history."* But, as I'd proven again and again, I needed a little push from time to time. Jeff Gorn pushed me to get my grades up. My brothers pushed me to get into Carroll. Coach Masonholder had to push me to take classes to stay eligible for football. Kelly gave me a push to commit (after I got a push to

Kelly Lange used to stop by my room when she was a resident's assistant in my dorm at Carroll College. I had met the love of my life, but it would be three years before we started dating.

break up with the other girl). We dated for about three months. We were getting pretty serious until I ran.

....

Kelly alone in courting ...

"I was with the Carroll College women's basketball team in California, and when I returned, he kind of blew me off. I thought it was weird. Then, I got really sick. I had mono(nucleosis). I even had to drop out of one of my courses. All this time, nobody even knew where Bob had gone. HIS brother actually called MY home asking where he was. The knucklehead had decided to get in his car and drive down to visit frat brothers in Miami. Personally, I think he was freaked out by his feelings for me."

....

When I got back, I didn't talk to her. We didn't talk for another three months. I was not a good guy. Then, we ran into each other downtown one night and reclicked right away. We've been together ever since.

For some reason I couldn't figure out, she took my undeserving, punky self back. I had disappeared on her as soon as we were serious. I told nobody where I went, including my supposed girlfriend. She was sick when I came back, and I never took care of her, brought her soup, checked up on her, asked how she was doing, NOTHING! What an ass I was.

Growing up, my parents gave me love when I kept screwing up. Now, this incredible woman was giving me love that I didn't deserve after screwing up some more. These were my first experiences with unconditional, undeserved, unrelenting love. I continued to receive it even while I, on the surface, seemed to only care about myself. On the surface—that's such an excuse. It's not on the surface that I seemed that way. It's how I really was. I cared about me.

The truth is—and I see this more now, in retrospect, than back then—I was the one person who really didn't love me at all. I felt so unworthy of the very feelings that kept me going on life's climb. I had found the love that God put before me in so many forms: parents, brothers, sister, coaches, friends, Kelly ... and yet, love for self was utterly lost on me as I continued to seek an ideal image, a great status, and personal fulfillment through food, alcohol, idolized roles, and, now, a prize woman on my arm.

·····························

It was around Easter in 1992. Kelly and I were living in an efficiency apartment, and she had left to visit her grandparents over spring break. While she was gone, I sat in that apartment by myself. I had always kept busy and social, but when I came back from my nights out, I was just used to her being there. I realized that I missed Kelly tremendously.

I didn't just miss her because she was good-looking. I didn't just miss Kelly because I was proud to have her as my girlfriend. I really missed HER … everything about her. I missed her gumption. I missed her humor. I missed her wit, which was far greater than my own (though she never made me feel like I wasn't smart). It may well have been the first unselfish feeling of my life. I couldn't stand her being away. I wasn't *me* without *her*. Immediately, I realized that this was the woman I couldn't lose. This was the woman with whom I wanted to climb every single one of life's cliffs. This was the woman I wanted to marry.

"You know what?" I said to myself. *"This is the one."*

Kelly was coming home on Sunday. I went out and bought a bottle of champagne and put it into the freezer to chill in time for her return.

When she came into the apartment, I sat her down and said, "We need to talk."

Kelly clearly was not thinking that this was a proposal. For all she knew, I had packed my bags for Miami while she was out of town but was giving her the courtesy of a goodbye this time! I sat her down on the couch and got serious, which wasn't much like me at all. She had to think this was "Goodbye."

"While you were gone, I thought a lot about our relationship and I have a question I have to ask you," I said. "Will you marry me?"

We were poor college kids, and I didn't even know until she had left that I didn't like the leaving part. This wasn't some big event that would have played out on YouTube for hopeful girls across the world to ooh, ahh, and dream about. I had no ring. I had nothing but an optimistic bottle of champagne waiting, but my optimism proved to be enough when Kelly gave me the undeserved gift of love yet again.

She said, "Yes."

When I went to get the champagne to toast with my new fiancée, it was frozen solid. We got to start off our future together with a good laugh.

....

A short while later, my fiancée and I were at a Milwaukee Brewers game. Kelly didn't have any beers. She was the designated driver, as I always made her be. There was no stopping me from the alcohol, so one of us needed to be responsible. Truth was, she really hadn't been drinking with me lately. She wasn't feeling great.

We were on our way home when she said, "You know, I'm late."

When I asked Kelly to marry me, I didn't have a ring and didn't even get down on one knee—even the champagne I had bought was frozen. But I knew that I never wanted to be separated from her again.

I wasn't scared. I wasn't even curious. I KNEW. I just had an immediate feeling.

"You know why?" I said.

"Why?"

"Because you're pregnant."

We stopped at a pharmacy on the way home.

Confirmed.

I guessed our engagement would be a short one.

In July 1992, we got married at Salem United Methodist Church, the same place where I'd been baptized and confirmed. It rained that morning. It poured! When we stepped outside at noon, though, the rain just stopped. The sun came out and it was beautiful! My mom cooked the food, including a tiered cake, which was leaning from the rain. Dad was our DJ, and I had captured her heart—

Kelly Lange Brenner.

Smart.

Hot.

Football Aficionado.

—and she'd captured mine.

....

Kelly's first glimpse into the man Bob would become:

"I remember it was New Year's Eve of 1992, and we were ready to ring in '93 with friends. I would rather have been home, to be honest. I didn't dress for the occasion. I was due with Kayla in February, so there I was in all my glory at seven months along, in my Chicago Bulls sweatshirt, at a New Year's Eve drunkfest.

We were at Bob's brother Brad's apartment with other friends. Everybody was drinking, except for me of course. Let's just say the party wasn't as funny to me as it was to everybody who was drunk. We stayed in, we played games, and everybody else drank some more.

Bob was already a big guy at this time, and he'd been drinking since he was a kid. To have a CASE of beer would be nothing to him. That's just a night in front of a game at home. It took an awful lot to get Bob to where he felt any kind of reaction to alcohol. And New Year's Eve is a celebration, so that's where he wanted to be. (Of course, anything could be cause for celebration to the man I'd married.) Most people would have had alcohol poisoning if they tried to keep up with him. That's just where his night started though. Mixed drinks were transitioned in, and Bob turned to his friend Jack Daniels.

I remember not feeling comfortable. I was tired. I needed to sleep in my own bed. That's all I wanted.

'Can we please just go home?' I remember begging him.

Nobody pulled Bob away from a party though. That's where he was the fun guy. Everybody loved him when Bob was drunk as a skunk, and that's where he was getting fast. Exhausted, I was trying to get comfortable in a bed I made on the floor. I was huge and relegated to the floor. I told him we should go home, and that's when he went ballistic.

'What are you EFFING talking about?!' (Fun Bob was the image for everybody else, but I got the jerk.)

'I am ready to have your child.' I cried.

I was emotional, exhausted, and confused about how he could treat me like this. Bob didn't THINK he was drunk. It was our classic role reversal. I needed to take care of him.

I finally just gave up, ready to sleep even away from home, ready to shut out this situation for eight hours. I told him, 'You're drunk. Please stop talking.'

He didn't though. Instead, he called me horrible names.

Stupid.

Slut.

Bitch.

And I can't even say it … the 'C' word.

The next day, I was hurt, crushed, distraught, and he acted like all was fine. He didn't usually have hangovers, so he'd wake up wanting to be all touchy with me and ready to start a new day. I put up with a lot of verbal assault at night, and he'd want loving in the morning! He was hateful, and oh, by the way, did I mention I was pregnant.

That night resulted in one of our biggest blowouts. It wasn't uncommon for us, if we were going out, to end in that kind of scenario. I wasn't a heavy drinker, even when I wasn't pregnant, and Bob was—Bob always was. It was hard for him—impossible for him—to ever admit that he was wrong, so I never got an apology. NEVER! I would be damaged, and Bob would act like everything was normal. I was supposed to be his wife and he the 'loving' husband.

I would almost have rather suffered a physical blow than the years of verbal blows. If it didn't work out, I could always say to somebody 'Well, he beat me!' Society would have told me I was right to get out of that situation. But when you're verbally abused … I was worried, wondering 'What would people think?'"

••••••••••••••••••••••••••

It was a quarter past three in the afternoon. Funny how we remember specific times for significant events. It's not like you say, "I went to the grocery store at 2:50pm on Tuesday." You would say, "I went Tuesday," if you even remembered the day. But our very healthy, ten-fingered, ten-toed, baby girl (whose gender we didn't know until that very minute), Kayla, joined us at 3:15 pm on February 9, 1993.

I admit I was a bit of a jerk. I had told Kelly that she didn't need any pain medication. She should have the baby naturally. She's a trooper, but it was just another example of my lack of compassion. That kind of attitude probably didn't help, but it was ultimately her choice.

I was 22.

Kelly was 23.

We had NO money.

I worked at the jail and was in school full time.

Kelly was making just $7 an hour.

We were *so* scared

BUT—

We were even more elated. It was incredible. It was our first child and I just cried. I had stood by Kelly during the delivery, holding her hand. We were these two young newlyweds … and then we were Mom and Dad. I remember wanting to kiss Kayla's entire face. She was so cool and so beautiful. You can't hold babies close enough.

So, yes. It was a quarter past three in the afternoon. That's when I became a dad and, once again, undeserved love was given to a man who felt unworthy.

After Kayla was born, the hospital took us through the process of caring for a newborn—like knowing how to change a diaper is going to handle the job! And when they cry? You're just supposed to learn what each cry means?

"I'm hungry."

"I'm cold."

"I'm hot."

"Hold me."

"Put me down."

"Pick me up."

"Put me down."
"Pick me up."
"Put me down."
"Pick me up."
"Where are you?"
"Where's my binky?"
"Where's Mom?"
And, oh yeah …
"I need that diaper change you learned about."

To me, they all sounded like "WAAAHHHH!" Panic set in. We were really parents. Bill Cosby said it best in his book, *Fatherhood:* "Having a child is surely the most beautifully irrational act that two people in love can commit."

Kelly and I got home mid-afternoon on the day she and Kayla could be released from the hospital. It felt a little like playing house at first.

We were in our marriage, sitting on our furniture with our baby, tired and cuddling. We only wanted to touch her and look at her. We weren't planning the future. We were just in the moment, appreciating her as a baby. We were ready for that Donna Reed ending where the two parents hug and kiss their new baby, tuck her neatly into a little crib, look at her dreamily from above; a strong husband with his arm around his wife who looks like she stepped not out of a hospital bed but a *Better Homes & Gardens* magazine.

For a moment, while we were in our little piece of it, all was right in the world. Then, at about 8 o'clock that night, we put her to bed.

Ha!

Kayla cried.

She cried and cried and cried, and I couldn't tell you which cry it was! Is she hot? Is she cold? She cried and cried. We rocked her. We talked to her. Did she want to be held? Is she hungry? We rocked her. She cried. We cried. She was inconsolable.

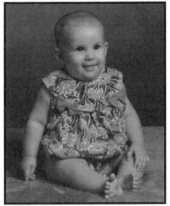

My daughter, Kayla, was born in February 1993. I was only 22 and Kelly was 23. It was hard, but I loved being a dad.

We were exhausted. Was she dirty? Was she lonely? She cried and cried and cried; Kayla cried non-stop until 5 o'clock in the morning. Far from *Better Homes & Gardens,* we looked like wanted posters! We were that over-exhausted, over-frustrated, and in over our heads. It's that kind of anger that just makes you want to scream or, at least, make the screaming stop. There was nothing we could do, or hadn't tried to do, to stop it, but I knew an expert who had raised six of these little creatures who turn your world upside down.

"Mom?" I phoned my mom in the morning.

"We haven't slept, Mom. Not in days. We need you."

My mom drove right over. Her Teddy Bear needed some mending. She brought Kelly and me breakfast and said, "Go to sleep. I'll take it from here."

And we did. And she did.

We were totally surrendered to sleep and went out like lights. Meanwhile, Mom took care of a bound-up Kayla, and our little daughter also went out like a light. Constipation! Already? I'm sure that was one of the cries we were supposed to remember.

Once the shock of being parents wore off and reality *set* in, we *settled* in, and I just remember being elated to be a dad. It was so neat in the baby years to have all those firsts—first word, first tooth, first step, and that first time they wave, "ba-bye."

Then, there are those times they wave, "hello." I would come home from working at the jail, and they would yell, "DADDY!" and I could kiss and love and snuggle them. That was the best time. That's when they started to grow up, of course. That's what was really my favorite time—when they started to walk and talk and express themselves.

I thought I was doing my part now, climbing toward more of what defined a great guy.

My son, Jordan, was born in 1994. Our children were the bond that helped keep our marriage together in the younger years.

I was a hard worker who brought home his paycheck.

I had the coach's beautiful daughter as a wife.

I was a dad who enjoyed all of those firsts and favorites.

I wanted to do even better, though, by being that great buddy, too.

The truth is that my image of who I should be had changed, but it was still just an image that I was portraying to the world while I hid the reality behind him. I was missing the call of my own family. Once the newness of Kayla wore off, I figured I had that role down pat, and now it was time to just be that new guy … Dad … while still majoring in my other roles as a friend, worker, and football coach. I didn't quit the coaching once I became a dad.

....

Kelly alone in need …

"Bob is an excellent friend. Anybody you talk to who is a friend to him will tell you that he is the guy who will be there for them. His friends took priority over our marriage and our child because, at that point in our lives, I wasn't a 'friend' to him. I was just the wife. Choices were made that meant he was still in that world of everybody else going out, drinking, answering their calls. When Jordan was born, I had him on the first day of football practice and Bob was coaching. He actually asked if I could be discharged around lunch so that it would be convenient for him to come pick me up. His family leave turned into football leave."

....

Even while I had more love in my life than I ever deserved, I kept this love of football. If I had days off, which rotated back then, I would try to do things with Kayla and Jordan, and it was always awesome. But, beyond that role of Dad, I would more often choose going out; Kelly would say I went out to excess. (She would have been right.) I went out for football. I went out for friends. I went out, and Kelly wouldn't even know when I would be coming back.

That didn't stop for a long period of time.

I was fine being Dad when "Dad" meant the cool cop, the football coach, the playmate, or that buddy everybody loved.

The title worked really well for the image I wanted to portray. I coached Jordan in many years of football, even his last when, like his dad, he tore his ACL. I talked to his team, and they all really respected me.

Being the cool dad doing the cool dad things, that was never a problem. When it meant that I had to be reliable and accountable, I didn't care enough to make those aspects part of my image. That part of the job wasn't part of my climb.

·····················

Maybe those early years, when I was a father only at my own convenience, are why Kayla and I didn't have a bond that was strong enough for the teen years. We began to butt heads the summer between middle and high school. I felt she was disrespectful to me and to Kelly. To be fair, things hadn't always been easy at home for any of us, much less a teenage girl. We always had financial troubles. My own actions were the main cause of all the marital issues we had over the years. We fought about them in foul-mouthed, unloving ways. Yet, like my own parents, who had to push through a lot of difficult times, Kelly and I were still together. We survived when a lot of marriages would have crumbled. I thought that deserved some sort of recognition.

Kayla's disrespect for Kelly was the biggest challenge for me, particularly during that period. I'm a guy. Guys operate on respect—that IS love to us. That sent me over the rail, and it seemed like I could never communicate with Kayla during and right after those teen years.

When I was on *Extreme Weight Loss*, the producers saw the drama in the relationship between Kayla and me, and we knew she would come across poorly to audiences. We warned her about the negative reactions she could get and told her not to be my doubter, but it was so ingrained in her.

Kayla was 16 when a lot of things started to go wrong in our home and our lives. I was about to change jobs with the department; I was a huge, unhealthy guy; we were slowly going bankrupt; I was about to surrender everything to God when my own kids didn't even know Him. If it hadn't been for that last piece, I would have reached self-destruction. Kayla didn't have that piece, so she only saw the self-destruction.

Was it too late?

Had I lost one of the greatest loves I'd ever found? I wanted to gain her back.

I.ntegrity Off-Duty

People with integrity walk safely, but those who follow crooked paths will slip and fall.

~Proverbs 10:9 (NLT)

There are some things I should share about drug work. It's no surprise that it's ugly, but it's not just ugly because of the people you're with and the things that, in their drug-twisted realities, they'll do to get the next financial or pharmaceutical fix.

My partner, Steve, and I had been working on the bust for a while. My alias was well-established. My name was Bob. Last names weren't shared, but it's sort of **Drug Cop 101** that you use some basic truths from your own life, especially your first name. It's important to avoid lies that you could confuse. Also, the worst thing a guy could do is turn his head when the wrong name is called out. An identity would crash down, if not immediately, then through the nervousness that follows. In that lost identity, you could lose months of hard work. Who knows what kind of loss could result?

"Undercover Bob" was the name player—the money guy in a deal we were putting together. "Undercover Steve" was established as my street-level dealer. For this deal, we were a package, working together on a $38,000 purchase of ten pounds of high-grade, California-grown marijuana.

Our best-laid plans included meeting our distributor at a park and ride, having him follow us to a storage facility where we supposedly kept our pot stash, excusing ourselves out to the car to get the money, and in the thirty-second interim, the SWAT team would arrive to make the bust. That bust would include us, of course. Usually, these busts happen so fast that the criminals don't pay any attention to what happens to the undercovers. We were their supposed co-conspirators after all, so their eyes are on the arresting officers (and the officers' AR-15, semi-automatic, full-trained weapons). Nonetheless, we would inevitably end up in the back of a squad car, cuffed and looking every bit as much the thugs as the guys we were taking down.

What is it they say about those best-laid plans?

Ours fell apart before they even began. Steve and I arrived at the park and ride and, in addition to our contact, he brought a driver. We didn't know him. Beyond the driver, we got some more company. This deal was just big enough that our contact's Milwaukee East Side supplier came as well … in yet another car … with yet another two unknown men. Now, Steve and I were outnumbered in vehicles and in people, including a supplier known to move hundreds of thousands of dollars worth of weed in our area. Suddenly, this deal became a much bigger deal.

Steve was wired and by my side, so in our own ways, subtle and otherwise, we made sure that our surveillance crews could hear all of this new information:

5 guys.

2 vehicles.

Big players.

We had ten minutes from the park and ride to the storage facility. It was enough time for the SWAT team to adjust their plan accordingly and split up for the final bust.

Steve and I hopped in our car to lead our contact. Your next lesson of **Drug Cop 101**: I popped open a bottle of Miller beer from an open 12-pack in the back seat of the Cadillac. Look the part. It wasn't about drinking and driving; it was about spitting in the face of authority. It's what the "money guys" do, so it was what I did. Off we went with our contact behind, and the other car following him. He was in our Mary Jane sandwich, the brain cells getting smoked out in the middle.

Here's another lesson of **Drug Cop 101** for you: There isn't one big, black van or a conspicuous plumbing or cable vehicle following us around with a mobile office of wiretap listeners for a bust of this size. Only Hollywood does things that way. We had about eight surveillance teams out with us on this drug bust. It's a good thing, too. With the supplier right there in the caravan with us, you can bet he was looking for followers, roadside vehicles with people sitting in them, too many cars, or a suspicious, parked vehicle in the area of our deal.

As we drove the distance between our two business points, one surveillance team would pick up our conversation and carry us for a short distance, and then pass the duty off to another car that would join the traffic flow, leaving the first surveillance team behind to turn off unsuspiciously. This continued all the way to the drug deal.

The storage facility was an open lot filled with 25 or 30 garages. Through the garages, there was a driveway that made an L-shape down the middle. At the top of the "L" was a 10-foot tall fence. This was a boxing-in if ever I saw one … or so I thought. We led our contact into the lot and all the way to the very back. We were at garage number 25, with just a few units left between us and the fence. We parked and our contact's driver pulled up next to us. I didn't feel threatened at this point. Between the piggy-backing surveillance teams and a nearby, well-hidden (well-armed) SWAT team, I had confidence we were covered.

The supplier didn't follow us in. Here's another tip of **Drug Cop 101**: Steve and I were pretty sure that the supplier was doing one of two things. Either he was driving circles around the block to check the area for surveillance, SWAT, or other police, OR he was parked at the entrance to the storage facility, keeping anybody out who may otherwise witness our exchange of money and drugs.

Steve opened up the garage, and our contact grabbed the drugs from his car. He didn't even need to pull out the pot for me to know what he'd be bringing us. **Drug Cop 101**: KNOW your product. There is nothing that smells like fresh, high-grade marijuana except for fresh, high-grade marijuana. Its pungency is very distinct. Its presence is very decided. Even at 9 o'clock at night, in a dark storage unit, I could tell you what was in the pillowcase he brought over to us. Still, we ironically pulled out a lighter, of all possible things, to pretend to check the quality of our merchandise.

Each of the pounds was individually vacuum-packed in clear plastic and labeled with its region of origin. As I stated, this was California for this particular buy. Funny thing is, drugs are also often stamped with a letter grade, like A, or AAA, or A+, like we're supposed to believe there's some sort of legitimate quality control agency (well, outside of Colorado anyway) that's out there testing street drugs for proper potency.

This one will partially fry your brain cells. This one will make you lazy and without purpose, but you'll be too high to care. This one will kill you slowly, but not before destroying your relationships. This one, though, has even been known to kill a few people quickly … now that's the good stuff!

"Potent pot. We're good, Steve," I said impressively, casually. That was it … my key phrase for SWAT to come bust the buy!

Okay, now it's time for some **SWAT Ops 101**: It's called dynamic entry. When a key phrase is called, you come in fast and hard on all suspects at once within 30 seconds of hearing the buzzword or code phrase. When there are multiple fronts, you split the SWAT team and each take a target. If you can't split up, you deal first with the main threat. Where there are drugs and there is money, you can bet there are guns. The deal was the main threat. Steve and I? We were in the middle of the main threat.

This is not how the arrest went down.

"I'll get the money," I told our contact. Steve stayed with him, supposedly to keep an eye on our purchase, but, in reality, to keep an eye on our target.

I didn't even expect to make it to my car before the bust would occur, but I walked casually over and … nothing. I had money in the glove compartment of the Cadillac. There were several stacks of money, and on the outsides of each stack were a couple of $100 bills. On the insides of each of those stacks were an awful lot of $1 bills. This money is for a quick flash, not a close look. You never want to have to pull this money out, but I was at the car and still … nothing.

"That was potent pot. Steve and I, we're good," I said to our contact's driver through his closed driver-side car window. I've left Steve behind WITH the drugs, WITH our contact (who is probably WITH a weapon) and still … nothing.

I had to buy some time.

"Hey, you wanna beer?" I said to the driver whose window was still raised.

"I'm good, man," he said.

"Crap! I'm going to have to get the money," I thought. I need more time.

"I'm going to have a beer quick," I said back, and I actually opened one up and started drinking it.

"Hey, you coming with the money?" Steve called, as aware as I was about the hot water we were in.

I reached into the glove compartment, setting down the Miller bottle, and grabbed my stack of not-going-to-fool-even-a-fool cash.

I turned around and saw Steve and my contact, gave my partner the *"Oh, Hell!"* look, handed him the stack and walked back to the car. I had to count on Steve to take care of himself from there. This was what he had trained for. We were keeping up appearances. This time the dark was our friend.

About five minutes had passed. It felt like an eternity, and while I wasn't worried for my life yet, this was definitely a bust gone bad. I needed to buy a little more time for Steve. Even though I didn't hear my SWAT guys coming, I didn't hear our contact's supplier either.

"Sure you don't want a beer?" I called to the other driver again.

As soon as I got that out of my mouth, I heard the SWAT team nearby … you couldn't NOT hear the SWAT team nearby! They were ripping the other three guys out of the car. They must have been blocking the storage entrance. They were screaming. It was loud and forceful with language and actions.

While that was happening, the driver of the car looked at me like he'd seen a ghost. I saw him lower the power window and turn his ear. "Is that the police? Did you hear that?"

We were only some seven feet apart from each other. I was at my driver's side door when I tried to brush it off, "You're hearing things."

I was watching him intently.

Steve was watching our contact.

The gig was up.

It was a done deal.

I was sure that our SWAT had split in two; some with the car and some with us, right? That's what they do! Except they didn't.

The driver I faced jumped out of his car, handgun in his left hand, and bolted for the fence fifty feet in front of us. It's funny how quickly a pothead can find his inner athlete when he thinks he might get busted.

Our contact pulled down the garage door to the storage unit, trapping himself, and any weapons he may have had, inside with my partner.

I drew my weapon and stood behind one of a narcotics officer's best friends, the A-pillar of the car door, and aimed at the runner. I assumed I'd be trapping the armed driver against the fence.

Instead, I watched the driver throw his weapon up on top of the storage unit and mount the fence as fast and furious as if it were nothing more than a hurdle! I stood there, needing to make my next move … get to my partner! Before I even took a step, the cavalry came around the corner! Detectives Steve Rudie (different Steve than my partner) and Vito Sorce were manning one of the surveillance vehicles when they heard everything go wrong. They didn't wait for the call; they simply recognized the threat and came to help.

"WHERE!?" they mouthed. (At least they understood the value of volume.)

"TWO!" I held up two fingers. "FIVE!" I held up five fingers and then pointed to the storage unit. " TWO-FIVE!" I mouthed.

With one detective holding an AR-15 directed at the door of garage #25, the other pulled that door open. From there, things went down as we had expected them to do before they didn't go down at all. Our contact was on the ground, sprawled out on his stomach with wrists cuffed behind his back. The same had happened with the supplier … off the streets … and his two sidekicks. My contact's driver was caught on foot, not far from the drug storage.

This was a day when we were more LUCKY than GOOD, but this was a good day of taking down bad guys.

You never know when one of those bad guys will have you in the dark with a weapon. You never know when one of them will discover a bundle of $1 bills sandwiched between a couple of $100 bills. You never know when you'll be left standing behind the door of a Cadillac filled with a 12-pack of Miller beer, all the time wondering if the guy running is going to turn back and shoot. You never know when your A-team won't show or when the cavalry won't arrive to sweep up behind them. Being in these conditions with these people are part of what makes the work of a narcotics officer hard.

Also difficult are the hours that a person must keep. There was no calling up the local drug dealer and asking him if he could please just please reschedule his next shipment so that I could make a softball game or a concert. Our friends called me "The Shadow."

It's the unpredictability of everything you do. Sure, there are those days when you get to sneak out and be "The Shadow" at your kids' events, but there are also days when the kids and wife are long since in bed while you're still out.

••••••••••••••••••••••••

Kelly alone in fear ...

"One night Bob didn't come home. I freaked out! 'You have to let me know if you won't be home,' I yelled at him. He told me that I should only worry if he's not home and the sheriff and a chaplain show up at the door. Otherwise, I shouldn't worry. He would either be home, or he wouldn't. It didn't help though.

I had absolute fear of him not coming home from work. I typically couldn't call him; he had to contact me because of what he was doing. The kids would ask where he was and I'd say, 'He's working.' We told them what he did, but I didn't think they needed to really know the dangers. It's not a safe feeling when you go to bed and you have no idea where your spouse is or how to reach them.

My coping mechanism was 'head in the sand.' I would go to bed and finally fall asleep, not knowing where he was. He would stagger in around three o'clock, and I would reach across the bed and feel for him. The amount of visual that was playing through my head until that time was everything that I had seen on television. Part of how I dealt with it was not discussing it. I would only get details when other people were over at the house and it would come up.

It was his way of protecting me by not letting me in on the details. With 12–18-hour days sometimes, he could actually have had a whole secret life, and I wouldn't have known it."

....

If the hours don't kill you or your relationships, sometimes it's the shady places where the work of drug users, abusers, and distributors take place. You go to them and make them your own hangouts. Kelly knew I went to strip clubs because that's where the business was, and she didn't worry about me straying, but it got old.

It's also the lifestyle that you have to adopt as your own when you're undercover. The things you do in your free time and the things you do "on the job" become one in the same. The guys we were around were all about internet pornography in their downtime and using or moving drugs in the rest of their lives. They talked a big talk with other men and flirted with any woman who looked their way. They wore expensive things to put on an expensive image. That became my image, too.

It's the ugliness that can come home with a guy who works in the narcotics unit … the mud on your boots when you come home from the work site. Whether it was from dealing with the criminals or dealing with the red tape we weeded through to capture those criminals, I know guys who permanently ruined relationships, lives, and their own well-being by bringing that crap home.

I thought I had avoided this piece of the dark work of drugs. I tried to check my "cop anger" at the door. But, even though I didn't think I was bringing home my work frustrations, I felt the same distrust for my family that I was used to having in the field.

There was a man who was working some of the downtown Waukesha bars as a known marijuana dealer. He had been in prison and was very paranoid, but I spent a lot of time with him and was able to gain some of his trust. Ultimately, I was able set up a deal with him. He was known for being dangerous and violent because of his paranoia paired with usually being high on something. This was not a guy you wanted to build a long-term relationship with. He wouldn't be a path to somebody bigger. We wanted a one and done: buy, arrest, and get him off the streets … fast.

I was getting ready for the bust.

Normally, I would wear a wire in a certain position. The idea of getting a mic on for surveillance wasn't something new. It becomes part of your uniform when you're undercover most of the time. You get used to what feels comfortable and stays concealed. For me, it would be on my chest or tucked into my waistband. At the last minute, I was thinking about this guy's paranoia. I decided I didn't want the wire in the normal place, so I cut a hole in my coat and wired it up from the inside. Even if he checked me, I didn't think he'd get into my coat.

I got to the bar where we would meet. He wasn't coming. I called him up, and he told me, "I think you're the police."

Pretending to be all enraged, I said, "I think you're the police."

That's when he told me I was being watched by somebody in the bar, and he thought I was talking to the guy next to me. Unlike actually being a cop, this accusation didn't fit. I really wasn't talking to anybody. This was his own craziness. We went back and forth until I told him I had the money. That did it. He needed it for his own fix.

He came in completely high on coke. I knew, based on his history, that it was one of his drugs of choice. He had the weed in his coat when he said, "follow me into the bathroom."

I knew what was going on. Trust was broken. It has a bit of a short life in my line of work. In the bathroom, he said, "I think you're a cop."

I responded, "I think you're an ass****."

He wanted me to take off my coat. I did, grateful that I had made the wire location change. I even had to lift my shirt. Getting into character, I started to undo my pants and said, "You want to effing check this, too?"

Finally, he backed off and took my money. Not two steps out the door, he was in cuffs and back in prison a short time after that.

Imagine that level of distrust toward others festering inside of you. Imagine that level of crudeness in communication slipping out in front of your wife and kids. Now, imagine not thinking that there was a damn thing wrong with those practices. That's where I was. As the Epicurus saying goes: *"The time when you should draw into yourself is when you are forced to be in a crowd."* I wasn't just in the crowd I was fighting; I became one of them.

Especially when you're working undercover and are forced to emulate the very life you're trying to eradicate, you can become consumed by the front you put on every day in the field. It's no secret that this is the life of a narcotics officer, a drug cop. The worse, the more violent, the more active, the uglier a city's drug scene is, the more restrictions they have on the (mostly) men who work in their narcotics units. In our Milwaukee metropolitan area, our officers weren't allowed to serve for more than two years. Most marriages don't last the stint, and it's usually because the spouses are tired of the life. Somehow, I served for seven. **Kelly served for seven.**

My appearance was foul. My surroundings were foul. My entertainment was foul. My mind was foul. My language was foul, adopting so many uses of the R-rated brother to "Flip," that I actually made another guy on the team uncomfortable. He made me realize I sounded like the guys I was busting. Even my soul had become foul. How could I climb toward anything great when I had fallen so far? How could I grow something good from this place?

Looking back, it makes sense that I, myself, was becoming foul. Matthew 13: 3b–9 (NLT) reads:

Listen! A farmer went out to plant some seeds. As he scattered them across his field, some seeds fell on a footpath, and the birds came and ate them. Other seeds fell on shallow soil with underlying rock. The seeds sprouted quickly because the soil was shallow. But the plants soon wilted under the hot sun, and since they didn't have deep roots, they died. Other seeds fell among thorns that grew up and choked out the tender plants. Still other seeds fell on fertile soil, and they produced a crop that was thirty, sixty, and even a hundred times as much as had been planted!

I was in the thorns, being choked out by the surroundings I had chosen for myself.

Even though I didn't bring home the attitude or the anger, I never really left the job. It becomes so much a part of who you are; it's like living a double life. The drinking didn't end when my shift ended; in fact, it often just began. The trips to "The Border" (the nickname given to a collection of strip clubs) became the same places I would frequent with my co-workers after hours. I was the biggest of the big spenders, stocking up on everything from my big Harley to the big, half-million dollar house I had to have built (despite being broke.) I knew the porn sites; I used cuss-filled language; I put on the flirt and followed strange women with my eyes. I was as much a thug as some of the guys I was busting, but my drugs were food and alcohol.

I thought that because I was good enough in my home and with my wife and kids, I had integrity off-duty. I had gained the trust of the dirtbags I was busting and was at risk of losing everything because of it. I was fooling myself, undercover in my own life, because, in reality, it was my integrity that *was* off-duty.

....

Paul Paikowski may remember me from the time he came into the drug unit, but I remembered him right off, too. He was a real character—a very traditional, tell-it-like-it-is, proud, Polish police officer. His skin was tough, but it was secretly wrapped around a soft heart if you could get him talking. We called him "Ski" around the office.

Ski's uncle had given him a Bobblehead Jesus. He had his own space, and because of some recent developments in his personal faith, he really wanted to show this thing off, so it was part of his locker.

Ski became the "religious guy" in the Waukesha County Metropolitan Drug Enforcement Unit, or the Metro Drug Unit for short, which consisted of officers from all of the surrounding police agencies, including Paul from the Waukesha City Police Department and me with the Waukesha Sheriff's Department. I, on the other hand, was called "Big Daddy." I was kind of guarded behind that title, but I definitely preferred it to being the Jesus freak, like Paul.

He had been with us a little more than a month when I was organizing one of my (he would say "infamous") trips to The Border. He had already been pulling away from the kind of life associated with the guys who work narcotics. *"Been there. Done that,"* was his attitude about the strip clubs.

I remember it was a Sunday night, and I asked him, "Don't you want to go? Are you in? Come on, what else do you have going on for a Sunday night?"

I kind of pestered him about it because I really liked Ski's company. We were friends. I wanted him along. Maybe part of me realized I was better behaved when he was with us. I did less flirting around him, stood up to those weak moments—not that I could have done much while saddled with that body. Paul thought, given the chance, I would have crossed the line. I was trying to fill a void.

Paul told me The Border was out. He was going to a Bible study group with his wife … and that kind of clashed with going to the strip joint. Still, he came along for a lot of our drinking sessions. We'd been out a few nights, and I was pondering Paul skipping out on The Border for the Bible. One night, at a Canyon City restaurant, I just asked him.

I had to know.

"Really, Ski? Bible study. And church? What's the deal? What's that all about," I played off like I was poking at him.

I had been sitting with two other guys, Gary and Bill, and I just jumped in and broached the subject. Paul shared a little about his "Jesus journey," and I could tell he was glad to sort of have an audience for this subject.

He had originally gone to what became his (and later, my) church with a cop's mentality. He wanted to check it out and not pull out his checkbook for something that seemed BS-laden.

There were times when we would be out on a bust, and Paul would be sharing a faith testimony or having a *literal* "Come to Jesus" meeting with an informant or even a guy he was arresting! We were often right there in earshot. We were on the periphery. We could hear. *I* could hear. Sometimes, I think he wasn't talking to the guy he was with at all—he was talking to me.

Paul never lied to me. He had no problem telling me when my integrity was off-duty. He was already my friend, my buddy. Ski was about to become one of my partners in defining integrity when off-duty. His invitation was the start of something much bigger.

F.aith in the Force

Faith is the confidence that what we hope for will actually happen; it gives us assurance about things we cannot see.

~Hebrews 11:1 (NLT)

In early 2009, I was about to lose the gig as a narcotics officer. It's supposed to be a gift after giving so many hours with so much inconsistency for so many years to such a dirty job. You have earned less dangerous work and less brutal schedules. It's a break and a well-deserved sigh of relief for the family that stayed beside a narcotics officer through all of the ugly, druggy mess. It still felt like a kick to the curb, a kick to the ego, and, ultimately, the kick in the ass I needed to get that ass in gear.

To make things worse, my son was growing up, and he'd be out of his high school football program soon, too; another one of my identities would be put on the shelf. Without narcotics and football, I didn't know what that left to describe ... *me*. I couldn't believe I was turning the page on that chapter of my work both in coaching and policing.

"Hey!" I was told by the powers that be, "You've been at this for seven years! You're long past your gate to get out. Somebody else can do this."

The transition was so hard. I was used to coming and going according to the work and the hours of drug dealers. Now, I had this accountability to be a 2:45 pm to 10:45 pm guy. I missed the independence and kind of being a bit of my own boss.

There was also a financial sock to my obese gut. We had anticipated the hit to a certain degree, but my paycheck was sometimes DOUBLED due to the necessary overtime to get the job done. Now? There was nothing extra. (And that "extra" was part of the budget to make the bills on all of those image-driven purchases over the years.) We turned to credit cards. Our debt grew and grew.

I used to love my job! Now, I was stressed with the hours and the new supervisory structure and not feeling compensated to make up for my loss. After all those years of my family not knowing if I'd be home at all, they got this new side of me, which may have made them wish I was just gone again. I was always irritable with a short fuse and long tirades. I was depressed. I drank. I ate from stress.

The stress eating didn't help with confidence on the job either. It was at this time that I grew to be my biggest ever. In my work with the Metro Drug Unit, I was supposed to look like one of the guys I was busting. I wore saggy jeans and big t-shirts that hung well below my waistline. Everything was loose and sloppy ... like me. Now, in slacks with button-down shirts tucked in at a belt with extra holes, the only sloppy thing *was* me. I couldn't even fit into a bulletproof vest. They don't make them the size of a guy who isn't fit for duty.

Worst of all, I no longer felt like I was making a difference. I used to deal with major federal cases involving prosecutors from all different levels—from local, to state, to federal. I was helping get really bad guys off the streets—guys who illegally carried weapons (the guys who would still have weapons regardless of the tightest gun laws), guys who acted out from drug hazes and psychotic needs to get high, guys who would take down their own sons and daughters and anybody in the way with them if it meant they got to line their own pockets, veins, or nostrils. I was helping to get the really bad crap they handed out to kids off the streets, too. All of it.

As a detective, I was always aware of the fact that there were victims involved, and I was sensitive to their losses, but most of those crimes are, to be frank, unsolvable. *"Why was your laptop stolen out of your unlocked car parked downtown on a busy night? Not sure. Maybe I should pull in the feds on this one!"*

The work was unchallenging. It was often unrewarding. I lost my self-worth. The difficulties I was having even led to a visit to the counselor I had to speak with regularly when I was a narcotics officer. (They like to make sure we're not falling apart ... I'm not sure I wasn't all those years.)

It wasn't just that I was losing faith in the force; I was losing faith in myself and all that I was supposed to be.

Who was I?

Leaving narcotics and leaving the overtime pay also meant that the house I was having built was suddenly and completely unaffordable. It meant the life I had been living no longer could be tolerated as part of the job. Suddenly, being the drinking, porn-watching, Caddy-driving guy who flirted relentlessly on late nights at the strip joints was anything but the *Big Daddy* title I carried.

Who the hell was I?

I'd had to redefine myself once before from football player to field officer. Now, all that was left waiting for me was family man ... the one role it seemed I had been running from my whole life by skipping out on the crowded family home of my youth for my buddy, Rob's, house, ignoring my sister, putting a new team before my newlywed wife, and being a financial provider rather than the fatherly proponent for my kids.

Even when I got to be the typical dad doing a career day or being my kids' coach, I was still in the role of football player or narcotics officer.

I knew how to be a football player. I knew how to be a coach. I knew how to be a cop. All these things were taken from me one at a time, so I asked myself:

Who the hell am I?

I felt like I had been climbing all my life only to be sitting still at the bottom of my cliff with a peak that was nearly insurmountable in my now larger-than-life-sized body. I had lost my identity and gained nothing but habits, addictions, and obesity. I needed somebody to throw me a rope.

Paul did.

It came in the form of an invitation to join him and his wife, Susi, at RiverGlen Christian Church. Kelly and I had both been raised Methodist, so this was a little different for us. The first time we went, we had to take in how different it was with a lot of contemporary music and a pastor, Ben Davis, who talked about real life today instead of just in a time more than 2,000 years ago. We didn't run away. I guess that was a start, especially for me. I didn't feel like Paul was drinking the Kool-Aid, so to speak.

Paul was my buddy on the force, and he was going to help redefine the force I put my faith into.

It was time I answered the question,

"Who am I?"

....

Toward the end of my stint with the Metro Drug Unit, I had built a good reputation as a reliable drug cop. Sometimes, the work we did would involve the Drug Enforcement Agency (DEA). Their resources were helpful, particularly when we crossed state lines. Our team had been working a bust that was about to go out of our jurisdiction, so this was one of those times when we would have to bring in the federal agencies. We brought the case to them and handled it collaboratively, with local, state, and federal officers.

I was working with a fellow Metro Drug Unit agent in California; we had been temporarily deputized by the FBI for this case.

The two of us were going to be out on the west coast for a few days, and I was taking advantage of the food, the hotel, and the drinks.

We went out that first day and ate like crap, drank too much, and stayed up too late. The next day, it was more junk for breakfast, for lunch, and drinking as early as we could. By the time it got to dinner that second day, my partner said to me, "Bob, I just can't eat and drink like this. I actually feel sick."

I was embarrassed.

I was hurt.

And I knew he was right.

But my pride kept me at the lifestyle for a little longer.

Another clash occurred between my faith in the force and the forces of food and alcohol that had continued to take a major role in my life. I was all set to work a contractor position in 2009. I was going to be embedded with a U.S. Army Division in Iraq. I was away from narcotics, and the desire to serve was still strong. What better way to do it than with those who serve all of us every day, as they fight for the freedom of others.

I already had top security clearance because of work I had done with the DEA. They needed me as an investigator, and they loved me. I had filled out all of my paperwork and was in conversations with the federal contractor who was going to place me. My resume was great. I had experience with the federal government and with wiretaps. We hadn't met though.

It came down to a call and that call came on a day in February when I was at Kayla's Kettle Moraine High School basketball game. I remember getting up from the stands to

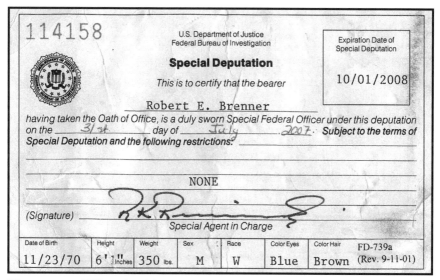

These are my FBI credentials. In 2008 we were collaborating with the FBI and a local Metro Drug Unit to take down a drug trafficking organization in northern California. When a fellow agent I greatly respected commented on the horrible food I was eating and the amount I drank, I learned the hard truth about myself.

take it. I was excited about the opportunity this call could mean, in addition to the fact that it would financially provide for my family.

We went through all the qualifications for the position. He told me about the work I'd be doing—honorable, hard work. Then, the question came up at last … the one I'd been dreading: "Tell me about your level of fitness."

I remembered the fit for duty trial that police with the Waukesha Sheriff's Department have to go through. I'm sure it's similar to what many departments have across the U.S. and in the federal government. At the time, I could still pass as far as actually completing the tasks, although the necessary timeframe left something to be desired by any service unit. The test required running a mile, including some weaving through cones, climbing both short and high obstacles, and ultimately pulling a dummy of average human weight and size out of a vehicle. No problem. We had to finish in 23 minutes. Problem. It wasn't lying to say I could do these things. Even as fat and out of shape as I was, I saw their tasks and knew I could complete them. I also knew, though, that this wasn't what he was really asking or looking for. Lives were on the line. He didn't care if I could weave through an obstacle course in some sort of maximum (or, honestly, beyond maximum) amount of time. I needed to be reliably fit.

"I'm a pretty big guy," I told him. "400 lbs. big." (And really, it may have been more at the time.)

He told me I would be in a uniform, in a platoon, and carrying another 50 pounds on my back in a military pack. I was going to be with that platoon, going on the treks, rather than in an encampment somewhere as I had first pictured. I wasn't going to be on the sidelines—on the perimeter; this was the offensive line—the stack—and our American soldiers would rely on *me* to protect myself and to look out for them.

We had a good conversation and they loved my resume, but I needed to be honest with myself … with the recruiter. I couldn't count on myself to be all that I could be when I was so much bigger than I should be. It wouldn't work right now.

"I'm not ready," I told him.

Maybe saying those words out loud is what told me that I needed to get ready. It was time to go to war with myself.

By December 2009, the drive to get back into drug work locally or as a contractor with the military was gone. "Our identity and our success go hand in hand," according to author Lila Swell. I felt as though I'd lost both and gained nothing but heartache in return. I was working now as a detective. The work itself felt humbling as I finally accepted the end of my career in nailing narcs. I could do the tasks though.

When somebody calls in a burglary, we follow up with the victim and show up to collect evidence. From the perspective of a person who has been robbed, I imagine it's frustrating. Somebody takes something from your home, so now you invite more strangers into your home to check the area that was violated. Often, because of that feeling, or maybe out of curiosity or the need to help, the homeowner kind of hovers as a detective investigates.

I was assigned to go to a home to take pictures, find fingerprints, and collect DNA. In this case, the homeowner had noticed an area where things were clearly disturbed. There was a handprint in dust on the floor, for instance. I got down on my hands and knees for the evidence collection, looking under beds and dressers, dusting for prints, and the like.

I remember getting on the floor, all 450 pounds or so of me, and my shirt had come untucked. All the while, the burglary victim was standing over me. I don't blame him. He wanted to make sure that I saw the areas that he had noticed from the robber's presence. I was sure I had the proverbial plumber's crack peeking out from the top of my pants.

What's worse is that, in the middle of this Wisconsin winter, I was sweating … profusely. When I finally stood, I had to ask him for a paper towel so that I could wipe my face. He got it for me and then the real kick came. Here I was, collecting evidence of a *crime* committed against this guy, and he gave *me* the "Man, I feel sorry for you" look. He had pity on his face … because I was fat. I wanted to crawl back under that dresser and hide.

Just like when my partner said he couldn't go on with my habits in California or when I had to turn down the contractor job I could have been great at doing, I stood in this stranger's house feeling ashamed. I was embarrassed. I, DETECTIVE Bob Brenner, was the victim AND the criminal in my own life.

I needed a new force to keep me going … to keep me climbing toward whatever the hell it was I was supposed to climb toward. Maybe the reason I wasn't in the same position to save lives as I used to be is because it was time I saved my own life.

I loved football so much that I even dressed up as a football player for Halloween in the 6th grade.

This was my 8th grade confirmation at the Methodist Church in Salem, Wisconsin. The suit looks pretty good for having been purchased for $2 from Goodwill! I wasn't taking my faith seriously at that point in my life.

Mom and Dad at my brother Bruce's wedding on August 21, 1999. It was sure great to see them holding hands and smiling in this picture.

I was 17 when this photo of the Brenner siblings was taken. (I am in front, to the left of my sister Becky.) We were all smiling, but I can assure you, once it was over, there was fighting (physical and verbal) between the boys. As my mom's only girl, Becky got put right up front in a dress, while the rest of us were in jeans.

My varsity year of football was my athletic breakout year. I received a lot of awards and accolades and my confidence grew. My senior year prepared me for playing at the next level.

After being overlooked by other universities because of my height and being ignored by the UW-Whitewater coach, I joined the team at Carroll College. It ended up being a great fit and I'm sure it was meant to be.

I was part of the starting lineup during my sophomore year at Carroll College. This was the year that I played my best football and reached the top of my C.L.I.F at that stage of my life.

When Kelly and I got married in July 1992, neither of our families thought it would last because we were so young and they knew how much I partied. They were right about the partying but, thankfully, wrong about us lasting.

My daughter, Kayla, was born while I was playing for Carroll College. Once again, my family was in the stands for me. It was a new generation but the same me.

Mike Schulz, who I played football with at Carroll College, asked me to be a groomsman in his wedding. I was working undercover at the time, so I didn't look too good (as you can see in this photo). I told him I wouldn't be hurt if he didn't want me in the wedding, but he wanted me there anyway.

Throughout my seven-year career with the Waukesha County Metropolitan Drug Unit, I helped seize hundreds of thousands of dollars in drug money and thousands of pounds of drugs as an undercover officer. Doing this required hundreds of overtime hours and time away from my family, but I felt it was what I needed to do for the job.

Being an undercover narcotics officer was how I identified myself, and I looked the part! I had always been clean-cut as a football player and coach and a police detective. There were no more grooming standards in the narcotics unit, and I took on the lifestyle of the guys I was chasing. I became somebody I wasn't.

I was blessed to be able to coach my son, Jordan, for many years of his student sporting career in football. It gave me an opportunity to be there as a dad for one of my kids. This is me coaching his 7th grade team.

During the Extreme Weight Loss *selection process, I met Johnny (in the middle). He didn't make the show and his weight and health got a lot worse. Less than a year later, he died from unexpected complications after hip replacement surgery. He was a really good guy who loved life but also a reminder to me of how that life could be lost if I didn't take care of myself.*

Photo courtesy of Mehrbod Mohammadi.

When the executive producer of Extreme Weight Loss, *Matt Assmus, challenged us to do push-ups, I took off my shirt and did five. I did it jokingly, but when it was done, I was shocked that I was able to do that many!*

Photo courtesy of Mehrbod Mohammadi.

All of the finalists were invited to CHLI at the Four Seasons Hotel during Finals Week. Only fifteen of us were selected to be on the show. Mehrbod, Mike, and I were some of the lucky ones. We are in the second to last row on the left.

Photos courtesy of Mike Epstein

I can't imagine three guys more different from one another than Mehrbod Mohammadi, Mike Epstein, and I, but we became lifelong friends and accountability partners, keeping track of each other during and after our Extreme Weight Loss transformations. Mike Epstein lost 221 pounds at the age of 50. He was originally told that he couldn't be part of the show because the producers were concerned about his heart, but he wouldn't take "no" for an answer. He was, for me, Chris and Heidi, the picture of perseverance. Mehrbod is one of the nicest, most loving and charismatic guys I've ever met, and he is like a younger brother to me. We are The Three Amigos! (Top right photo, from left to right: me, Mehrbod, Mike)

My dog Walter loved me before and after my transformation. He's my buddy!

My final weigh-in took me back to my alma mater, Carroll University, in May 2013. I weighed just 195 pounds and had lost 56% of my body weight, the most out of any man in the history of the show, but my eyes weren't on the numbers. My wife was in the front row of the audience, and I was looking at her, filled with gratitude.

Photos courtesy of Andy Drefs

My family and Chris and Heidi Powell were my cheerleaders throughout my year of transformation. Bruce and I did sprint triathlons together. My parents called every week to find out about my progress. Both Mom and Kelly got on board and went through their own weight loss transformation. And, for the Wounded Warrior Project, my entire family raised $7,000 and supported me as I swam across the lake.

Rob Hall (front left) surprised me by getting people from our 1988 high school class to join him at my finale.

The old Bob would never have thought of doing hot yoga because it's not a "manly" thing, but it turned out to be an incredible tool for my weight loss. I burned between 1200-1500 calories per session while also building strength and learning to stretch.

Bruce and I finally found something we could do together: sprint triathlons. Just three months after I joined Extreme Weight Loss, we did the Tri-Rock triathlon together. I beat him in the swim, but he beat me across the finish line. Bruce then came back to get me so we could finish the race together.

Lucky to be healthy enough to spend Father's Day with my dad in 2014. Glad to be enjoying good weather, good times, and foods that are good for us.

Here I am working out with the associate producer of my episode of Extreme Weight Loss, *Kerry Shanahan, three months into my transformation. We climbed a mountain at Arizona State University. She was my contact person, and she also became my lifelong friend. Kelly and I flew her out to Wisconsin to be part of my finale.*

Kelly and I took a hike at one of our local parks in the city of Waukesha the summer after my reveal episode. Kelly had joined me in my fitness program and ended up losing 50 pounds.

Kelly and I joined friends for yoga in the park. These photos signify our new future of spending more quality time together that also includes exercising—not just hanging out at the house!

I was invited to go on Windy City Live, which is a regional talk show in Chicago, to talk about the Season 5 casting call for Extreme Weight Loss *in February 2014. I gave some tips for people coming to the casting call: come with an open mind and open heart and be open to the process of transformation.*

Kelly, Jordan, and I were invited to meet Donald Driver before the filming of Season 4. He played for the Green Bay Packers—I let him know that I'm a Bears fan (his big rival), but he was still a great, stand-up guy with us!

Celebrating our 20th year wedding anniversary in Paris, France. Little did Kelly know she would receive diamond earrings 5 minutes later!

Kelly and I taking a selfie on the "love lock bridge" in Paris. What an amazing trip! So blessed!

My friend and producer Tom Becker, Chris, and me at the start of our bike ride in Rambouillet, France.

Chris and I have a tricep "flex-off"! I think he won!

Chris and I taking a quick break from our biking journey. I will never forget riding stage 20 of the Tour De France with my buddy!

Kelly and I took this photo while we were exploring the streets of Paris. We were on our way to the big white church on a hill, Sacré-Coeur.

My friend, Rob Hall, travels all around the country these days in his real estate work. This picture of him from 2013 hanging out on the edge of a cliff is one of my favorites. It reminds me that my lifelong buddy is on my climb with me.

Photo courtesy of Rob Hall

Kelly's Perspective

I remember going to Germanfest one year. Wisconsin was a state that really built up during the Industrial Revolution era, so there are all these pockets of the old European immigrant communities, and every one of them has a festival: Italianfest, Polishfest, Irishfest, a few I'm probably missing besides the music-packed Summerfest, and—for much of the state's heritage—Germanfest (not to be mixed up with Oktoberfest even though they are essentially the same celebration). Whatever the fest, they could all be called Foodfest and, more likely, Beerfest.

We went to Germanfest every year with as much family as we could get together. One year, the kids weren't with us, and we went down to the celebration at the beginning of the day. We spent all day there and well into the evening. It took a majority of that time for Bob to make his way toward drunk. I could tell when he was getting to that line between a fun drunk and a mean drunk; he was getting there that day. I just remember telling him, "You need to slow down."

We were with his entire family, including Becky, who had brought the man who would eventually become her husband. I hated when he'd make himself into a jerk, and I'd come out looking like I had no strength for putting up with him. I would often tell him when it was time to ease off (to not cross that line) and that would be his "You can't tell me what I can and cannot do" moment. Then, to stick his point—I don't know, I guess he thought it was masculine—he would bulldoze full throttle over that line.

Sure enough, he was in mean drunk territory, and I was in "protect our images" mode. I was trying to get him out of Germanfest. Bob decided he needed a bag of those cinnamon nuts as we were leaving the festival. Finally, I got him to the car. He was pissed and he started eating in that anger. When I say he looked like a pig eating these things, I'm not kidding. He was shoving handfuls in his mouth; they were just falling all over him. It was not attractive. Then, he was throwing the bag.

I remember saying again, "SLOW DOWN." And again, whenever you gave Bob a command, he would THROW DOWN and do the exact opposite. My command pushed him, and he called me an "Effin C-word," again.

I remember thinking, this is not right. This is not what marriage should be. But what could I do?

There are a couple reasons I never left Bob. First of all, I just didn't want to give our parents and all the doubters the satisfaction of being right when they had said, "it'll never last." I guess, in my own way, that made me as stubborn as he was. More importantly, I was so afraid of what would happen with the kids. Because of his friends and his position, he was thought of very highly and respected very deeply. Who would believe he was this other man? You think you'll have to lay your story out there for the world to defend your position, and nobody wants to do that. They would think I was a bitch to leave him … everybody. He was this jubilant, larger-than-life personality to everybody else, but, in the background, he had the potential to be a very mean-spirited, ugly person. He even threatened me once that if I left, I was never going to get the kids. I had no choice but to believe him.

During the narcotics years, because of his size and tolerance and what he could "handle," I didn't think he'd get himself killed from alcohol poisoning or driving drunk. For me, it was just that I never knew how far he would go with his viciousness. I also had a really hard time reconciling how to be intimate with somebody who was just so horrible to me over and over again. I always figured he was used to growing up in a house with parents who screamed and swore. Since my parents weren't like that, I just needed to be compassionate.

In 2009, Jack Daniels came back into Bob's life. It was the end of Bob's drug stint, and it should have been a family celebration. I was the one who had to keep everything together when he was working in narcotics. He wasn't okay with leaving the unit though. For him, he needed to eat and drink to forget, not to move on. He had a going away party at a downtown Waukesha bar. It was packed with probably more than a hundred people. It was a Friday, and on the following Monday, Bob would be starting as a detective. When the alcohol came out, so did mean Bob. I wanted him to have his goodbye, so I just left. I couldn't even be there to help close that chapter in his life … in our life. I knew I'd have to deal with him in the morning.

Later that night, I guess one of the guys saw Bob walking around the streets of downtown Waukesha looking for his car … even though he had been driven to the party. Bob gave the guy wrong directions, but he remembered where we lived and got him home. I remember him coming in, and he passed out before making it to the bedroom.

I thought, "Oh great, he's going to pee in the hallway." The kids were older at this time. I couldn't hide that sort of thing from them anymore. I heard him stumbling around and didn't know if he was going to get a drink of water. Then, I heard the front door shut.

I flew out of bed and found him on the front porch of the house, buck naked, all 400 pounds of him, peeing off the front steps. I was trying to pull him inside. What if the kids saw him? What if ANYBODY saw him? I was worried for our livelihood. I was worried for so many reasons. Needless to say, his verbal blows were rolling and rolling. I was dumb. I was stupid. I was every curse word under the sun. Finally, I got him in. We both crashed, angry.

I was never really good at softening the next day.

I was hurt.

I was pissed.

I gave him the silent treatment. The wall of silence those days was lasting longer than it had when we were younger. With each episode, I started building a wall.

Typically, after his drunken episodes, he would end up passing out. I can't tell you how many times Bob would just pee in the middle of the room or in the bed because he thought he was in the bathroom. I would have to clean up after him. It was my husband, but it was like taking care of another child right when I was supposed to get him back from that disgusting world of drugs.

Bob was an unbelievable friend to people at the expense of his marriage. They all got the fun Bob. But me? I got to clean up the sheets after he pissed in our marriage bed … in more ways than one.

I was done.

I had lost my husband and needed to do something to gain back my own future. I was really waiting until the kids were old enough so that leaving Bob wouldn't affect my time with them.

Thank God something far better happened before that time came …

C.L.I.F. Notes

Remember the first time you got to lead something? Responsibility has a way of making a person feel like the journey is done and the reward is at hand. Maybe it's when you start that college application process? That is such an "all-grown-up" kind of moment in a person's life. Then there's actually graduating. You feel like you're THERE! Or, starting college? That's kind of like actually hearing that over-enunciated, female, computer-animated voice saying in your ear, "You have reached your destination." Of course, you laugh at that voice years later when you realize it's that first grown-up job that *really* tells you "You have arrived." Or, is it when you get married? Maybe it's not until you own your first home or hold your first child?

All I know is that all sorts of things that happen *before* the big milestones are filled with lessons and leaders—lessons to teach you how to make life's climb and leaders to show you what to do when you get there. We get all of these great C.L.I.F. note tips for the times that are just a warm up for *real life*. Then you get to the actual milestones, when you could honestly use the help, and you feel kind of stuck out there in the wind. All of a sudden, you're supposed to BE the lesson and BE the leader, but you're just kind of lost.

Theme: Believing in Nothing

When I think about how quickly life happened for me, I realize that I never took the time to absorb all that I was given and everything that I was so lucky to have. I had a family, a great education, and a job, but my commitment was to the same kind of ugly lifestyle of the creeps I was cleaning off the street. How did that even happen?

I was moving from pouring my commitment onto the football field to pouring it into field work. Meanwhile, I was missing my most important mission field of all—my wife and kids. I was always chasing something beyond what I already had in front of me.

Lessons in Commitment:
- **Commit to the gifts you HAVE.**
- **Give time to what you value.**

In retrospect, I spent a lot more of my time—my COMMITMENT—living the life I was trying to eradicate than living the life I was given to appreciate.

> *Commitment meant nothing; providing money without providing love.*
> *I misunderstood what I really needed to provide my family.*
> *I needed to help.*

Symbolism: On the Edge with Me

Again and again, I learned the words, "Love ya, Buddy!" I would say them to friends, but it was hard with my family, The people who deserved to hear that sentiment most of all. I thought I showed them love just by financing a life for them and being a hard worker, but when I got moved from narcotics to detective work, I didn't even have that anymore.

I felt like a failure. I had made a commitment to my work and that commitment was meant to take care of the people I loved. Kelly stuck by my side through all of it. I was saying words of love to friends and never to her. Now, I thought I'd lost the ability to give actions of love to her, too.

Lessons in Love:
- **Remember words of love.**
- **Remember actions of love.**

Kelly was there with me on the edge. She was there when the money was gone, when the house couldn't be built, and when even my huge frame couldn't hold me together. She did it all! I needed to redefine what love meant and redefine how to express it. Kelly loved me when I didn't love myself … and I thought *my* job was risky.

> *Love meant nothing; empty words to the wrong people from a broken man.*
> *I misunderstood love from the same heart that acted in hate.*
> *I needed help.*

Lifestyle: Hanging Off the C.L.I.F.

At the end of this chapter in my life, I felt overstuffed and underfed. Hundreds of pounds of emptiness. I've got no right to try discussing integrity based on a time in my life when I couldn't even recognize it myself. I couldn't have found it with a wiretap. In retrospect, though, I see that it was there in those around me. People kept falling into my path to address me with courage and honesty about who I was and who I wasn't.

I saw integrity when Ski told me he couldn't come out to the strip club.

I saw it when my partner told me that the way I ate and drank made a person sick.

I even saw integrity when I was told, "Hey! You've been at this for seven years! You're long past your gate to get out. Somebody else can do this."

When I started putting my hurt ego aside, I also saw integrity in the work I did as a detective. I remember one case, in particular, where a couple of heroin addicts burglarized an elderly man in a suburban subdivision. They stole a Canadian citizen's driver's license, credit cards, a visitor's visa, and a passport. Most important to the man, though, was his camera.

When I got a lead that there were heroin addicts involved in the case, based on my experiences with the drug scene in the area, I knew who they were. It was a couple and the guy was already in jail. I met with the girlfriend. I was able to honestly say things like, "This wasn't you. It was the drugs." *(Ironic how easy it was for me to see this in others.)* I showed compassion to her, so she showed me a willingness to talk. Ultimately, the girlfriend gave me a multiple page confession. I recovered the elderly man's camera, and it meant a lot to him. I made a difference that day to that man.

Lessons in Integrity:
- **Recognize purpose.**
- **Put aside your ego.**

Everything a person does in life prepares that person for the rest of life. I may have been in a bad place. I was feeling broken to bits at the bottom of my cliff, but I had still done good things. I was going to have to start using those things to put humpty dumpty back together again.

> *Integrity meant nothing; mine was non-existent.*
> *I misunderstood how to be a good man.*
> *I needed help.*

Character Insight: About Growing Me

With every pound I gained, I wasn't just feeding my weight, I was feeding all of the negative things in my life … all of the wrong things. I was a drunk on bad choices, and like a drunk, one bad choice didn't quench my thirst, it just grew my tolerance.

I know what it is to look in the mirror and hate what you see.

I know what it is to take that hate out on others and to be too damn prideful to admit it when you do.

I know what it is to feel like you have no value as a husband and a provider.

I know what it is to not feel worthy of protection. I didn't even care about the time when I wasn't able to strap on my bulletproof vest over my mass. I just didn't care.

I know what it is to feel shame … hurt … embarrassment … pain … guilt … regret.

I have felt all those things.

To make it better, I turned to food.

I turned to drinking.

I turned to spending.

Then, I'd hate myself more and turn to those things for more unattainable comfort.

I had spent my first forty-some years building ME, and it didn't do me a flippin' bit of good.

Here's the thing. I never understood that whole "over the hill" at forty years old thing. Forty can actually be a pretty good number. Noah sat through forty days and nights of rain, but he got a rainbow. Moses sat on a mountaintop for forty days … twice … but he got to talk to God! After forty years of wandering in the wilderness, the Israelites got to the Promised Land.

There were great promises waiting for me, too.

Lessons in Faith:
- **There is always hope.**
- **Every person has worth.**

  Faith meant nothing; I needed to find it.
  I misunderstood everything I had ever been.
  I needed help.

So many things were at play in my life, but all I could see was the cliff I had been on. This was the climb for me. Growing up, the idea was to get big to get on the line. Get on the line to get the win. Get the win to tell people I'm worthwhile. Tell people I'm worthwhile, so that I can surround myself with them instead of thinking about who I am. If I'm one of the worthwhile, cool people, I also get to go out to drink. A lot. Eat a lot. Drink a lot. Climb toward some ideal image that I had in my head for who I was supposed to be.

I wasn't making good choices in my climb, and I was putting a lot of weight on each step I took, but this was my identity, so I didn't know any different. I was committed to that image. After that, even though my surroundings had changed, going from high school to college and then college to work, I was still working toward an *image*.

In college, I kept eating and drinking my way toward becoming the big man on campus. I loved the game whether it was the game on the field or the game I was playing at to keep this identity going.

Then, when I became a cop, I didn't just want to work the traffic scene. I wanted the prestige that came with one of the toughest jobs. I became a narcotics officer and worked the drug scene. The image lived on because, when you're taking down really bad guys, you get this idea in your head that you can only be great if you're even *badder* than they are. You're tougher. You're bigger. When the scene took me to the bars, to the clubs, to drinking and driving, to foul places with foul people, that's where I went. Then, to let it all go at the end of the day, I'd take my guys back out to those same places. I didn't even know it when it was happening, but what started out as integrity for the job, turned into a total LACK of integrity in my life.

Life was getting heavy up here, and so was I, but if there was something bigger than my wardrobe when I was at my biggest (and my lowest at the same time), it was my pride.

It's an easy trap to fall into in our culture. There are so many symbols and material things that are supposed to measure our worth and not one of them has to do with admitting our weaknesses.

When celebrities go into rehab, we mock it in the media instead of cheering them on for getting help. The man who has the well-paid job, coaches his kid's football team, and still "finds time" to go out with his guy friends every night and weekend is seen as having the life without regard for how much time he's spending on his home or his marriage. Why are we celebrating life's poor decisions, and, what's more, why are we afraid to ask for help?

What would be wrong with a man saying, "I'll have to call it a night, guys. I gotta get home"?

What's wrong with saying, "I can't do it alone"?

I couldn't do it alone.

I couldn't do it alone.

I was a morbidly obese alcoholic failure, and I couldn't do it alone.

I tried every fad diet out there. I'd lose 50 pounds and gain back 100, and it wasn't just the weight. For me, just like at a buffet, I saw the things that were suggested for my meal, and I wanted ALL of them. In life, just like in eating, I put it ALL on my plate. Houses, Harleys, and hangouts made me into a cultural hero, and Kelly was the one who had to catch me every time I fell off my white horse.

We're measured by how well we can hold our alcohol. I held mine, and much to the dishonor of my family, I did that on my own, taking time away from them.

So I was killing my relationships!

The riskiest job is a status symbol. I wanted it. I got it. And I worked to keep it for longer than a person is supposed to be able to because I knew best.

But I was killing my integrity!

The biggest house was on my wish list. I could do it even if the bank said I couldn't. I knew best.

But I was killing my finances!

Our society worships the biggest guy whether on the team or on the streets. I wanted to be that guy, and, more importantly, I could do it on my own.

But I was killing myself!

I should have been proud. I climbed the cliffs that life had to offer because I thought that the view from the top would make me king of the mountain. When I got to the top, though, all that was waiting there was the real me: a 450-pound guy with a whole lot of excuses, a whole lot of lies to myself, and a whole lot of self-loathing—and I was losing my balance.

This wasn't a proud man! This was a prideful man! I didn't have faith in myself. I didn't have faith in anything! And I sure as hell couldn't expect the people who I'd hurt the most to have faith in me. This cliff ended in a capital "F" for "FAIL."

Who wins in this kind of climb? Who is waiting at the top of this kind of cliff? How long can a person hang on? How long could *I* hang on?

When I look at the pictures of me at 450 pounds, I'm reminded of all the things that were weighing on me besides my morbid obesity and realize I was never at the top of the cliff; I was hanging off of its edge, clinging on for dear, sweet, undeserved life. I don't know how many people I would destroy as they broke my fall.

We don't talk about pride and how negative it is in our lives. I was finally over my pride. Finally, I was smart enough to see my addictions to food and alcohol and how these things were ruining every aspect of my life. I needed help with food and nutrition. That's what everybody could see, but those were just the weaknesses that were on display. Those were the fails that everybody noticed. I hid all the other things. The weight was really an addiction to food. I was an alcoholic. My relationships were hanging on by a string ... and my pride was holding a pair of scissors to that string.

Suddenly, I looked at the entire world through different eyes. I had this building desire inside of me to not just help myself but to help all the other people hiding behind their images up on their cliffs. Most of all, I wanted to help the people I loved, who had undeservedly helped me for so long.

I was about to be introduced to Paul Paikowski's favorite book, but even before I began to work in it, it began to work in me. Isaiah 43:19 (NLT) tells us:

> For I am about to do something new. See, I have already begun! Do you not see it? I will make a pathway through the wilderness. I will create rivers in the dry wasteland.

I was *in* the wasteland, hanging in the wind without lessons or leaders. My failure was complete, and it began with addiction. The addiction was food and alcohol and selfish pride. I needed to make a choice between a life of addiction and ... simply ... LIFE. I was ready to drop the FAIL from my cliff and that meant it was time to drop my pride. Surrendering *control* of my life in order to *regain* my life was my first step.

For once, I was ready to make a bigger impact than my clothes.

Extreme and Unstoppable
What They Meant When Growing Me

During my growing years, it was my lifestyle that was extreme. Drinking, long hours, strip clubs, and big drug busts characterized a majority of my time spent. During those times, I ate and ate and ate, making my weight and my hate the unstoppable factors in my life.

My image was also extreme: the cop, the buddy, the football coach.

My selfishness was unstoppable. I was keeping up appearances instead of keeping up on budgets, being the fun guy instead of the reliable husband, and laughing off the weight that could kill me.

I was extreme. I was unstoppable. And I was on the path to a soul that *would* break at an early age if I didn't apply those words to other areas of my life, gain something besides failures, and lose something besides myself.

PART III
Transformation—
Growing My World

We can rejoice, too, when we run into problems and trials, for we know that they help us develop endurance, and endurance develops strength of character, and character strengthens our confident hope of salvation. And this hope will not lead to disappointment …

Transformation:
What They Said

Jesus said, "Blessed are the pure in heart" (Matthew 5:8). And the message of the Beatitude is a clear one. You change your life by changing your heart! Society says change the outside and the inside will follow. [...] But peel away the layers, and underneath you see our true nature: a selfish, prideful, sinful heart.

Jesus said, "I tell you the truth, unless one is born again, he cannot be in God's kingdom." (John 3:3) At our "new birth" God remakes our souls and gives us what we need. New eyes [...]. A new mind [...]. A new vision [...]. A new voice [...]. And most of all, a new heart!

**~From *The Applause of Heaven* and *A Gentle Thunder*
by: Max Lucado**

BRUCE SAID:

"There was always a worry obviously. When he was big, I looked at my wife and said, 'I don't know how much longer he's going to be around.' He'd start a crash diet—put a drop of medicine on his tongue and eat 4 ounces of meat. It was crazy."

ROB SAID:

> *"After that ten-year break, it was sad to see that he'd gotten so big. To hear his stories about stakeouts and drive-through eating was sad. He was self-conscious about it. It was a vicious cycle. He'd say,'I'm big. It is what it is.' I felt bad for him, but I didn't see him enough to really push. Instead, I'd joke back with him, 'Hey buddy, you look great. More to love.'"*

PAUL SAID:

> *"I could obviously see that he wasn't healthy. I remember being out and shaking down a drug dealer. We had to walk up this hill. He was going up the hill to pull some marijuana and was out of breath. I actually thought he might die climbing that hill. And, when my family went to visit my mother-in-law in Germany, Bob had us bring home a four-foot long shoehorn so that he could put on his own shoes. It was sad."*

JOHN PIETENPOL SAID:

> *"I had worked with Bob once to lose weight. He left me at 350 pounds after we had worked together for six weeks. He contacted me six months later to give it another try, and he came in weighing 450 pounds. He had gained 100 pounds in six months."*

HEIDI POWELL SAID:

> *"I remember when we started to work with Bob, we kind of doubted all of the older guys, but especially Bob. He was so strong-willed. He was a cop and a coach, and I didn't know if he could change."*

JORDAN SAID:

> *"It was fun when he was big, but it was sad to see him lose all that weight and then gain it back. I didn't realize how big he was because he was a strong guy. I didn't realize how really, truly big he was until I looked back. We could have lost him."*

ROB SAID:

> *"I remember phone calls with Bobby when he was getting excited. He had tried to get into various weight loss shows. He'd be excited and then get defeated when he didn't qualify. It was a roller coaster."*

KELLY SAID:

> *"I did not want to think about what this family would be like without him."*

PAUL SAID:

> *"I told Bob, 'God found you in the hole. It's time to get out of the hole.'"*

....

There are two pieces of paper that changed my life.

No.

That's not right.

There are two pieces of paper that ~~changed my life~~ SAVED my life.

First, I filled out this card:

baptism

__ I would like more information about becoming a Christian.
__ I have questions about baptism.
__ I am interested in being baptized in the next baptism service:

Saturday, November 13th, 2010

__ I would like to arrange another time for my baptism.

Name_____

Phone_____

Email_____

Best time to reach me_____

**Please place this card in the offering bag or turn in at the Information Center & a staff member will contact you.

Photo courtesy of Charity Miller

Being baptized in November 2010 was the beginning of my transformation. My heart was already there. The baptism was a way to publicly pronounce that I had decided to follow Christ.

Then I sent this letter:

March 8, 2012
Chris,

I wanted to start out this letter by telling you how humbled I am to be writing to you. It is so powerful to think about a true lifesaving, life-changing opportunity that is before me. I am a fallen man with my weight, and I need someone to pick me up and lead me to health and happiness.

I'm over 40 years old, and by all accounts, I have a wonderful life. I married my college sweetheart (Kelly), I am the father to amazing children (Jordan-17 and Kayla-19), and I have the job I have always dreamed of doing since Ms. Fox's third grade classroom—be a cop. I was a successful high school and college athlete and have more friends than it is legal. Most anything, I have set my mind to challenge and succeed, I have. But, I have failed miserably in two areas of my life: diet and exercise.

When I finished football in 1993, I stopped lifting weights and running. I continued to eat food like I was at the buffet every day. As my weight climbed out of control, I always sought out a cure. I started with "slim-fast," then diet pills, soup diets, Weight Watchers, HCG, and starvation diets. Each time I dieted, I would spend months losing weight only to spend only a couple months to gain all the weight back and then some. I'm sure you have heard similar accounts from your clients.

I was reminded recently by my orthopedic doctor that I need my left knee and left hip replaced in the future. He said the replacement process would be tough due to my size. It was his polite way of saying I have to lose weight in order to have the replacements. More critical to me is my livelihood.

If I am being honest with myself, I can't effectively do my job anymore. I would be hard pressed to subdue a violent person during the course of a criminal investigation. I couldn't run to help a fellow officer in need due to my weight. I definitely couldn't complete the "fit for duty" exercise required of our new officers. In addition, my secondary job as a football coach has suffered as I cannot instruct the way I did so previously. I am very sore after games and practice and don't know if I can do it any further. I love the sport of football, it is my passion.

Chris, I know you want to help people who want to help themselves. You also want to be around people who will be thankful for your mentorship, friendship and your compassion. I am one of those persons. If you give me the opportunity to work with you, I will NEVER give up. I know you will push me and at times I won't like it, but at the end of the day, you will be glad you gave me a chance. I won't let you down and most importantly, I can't let my family down. I love my family and would die for my family. They are also reaching out for your help through me.

Thank you for reading my letter. It would be my honor to work with you. I hope to meet you soon and if I do, expect a bear hug from the big man!

Sincerely,
Robert Brenner

I was broken in so many ways that went beyond my weight, and I needed, more than anything to be healed so that I could begin to heal the relationships and failures in my life. I needed to use my brokenness to build anew. Most of all, I needed to hold on tight. My transformation—the end to my forty years in the wilderness—was about to begin.

C.ommitment to Good

In the same way, let your good deeds shine out for all to see, so that everyone will praise your heavenly Father.

~Matthew 5:16 (NLT)

Lance Armstrong (before he admitted to blood doping, of course) made famous the quotation turned book title *It's Not About the Bike*. He was talking about his fight for life against cancer … a fight he won. I get that. Don't misunderstand me. I'm not putting myself into the same category as people fighting cancer, but I understand fighting to make a comeback, and I understand when it's not about the job and it's not about the competition

It wasn't about the weight loss for me; it was about the life I could have after the weight loss. It was about the family I could love back. It was about the purpose I could serve. It was about a journey that began before the weight transformation did, and that required the weight transformation in order to see it through.

When Paul Paikowski's invitation to join him at church came around, I didn't really have much further to fall. I was bankrupt, financially, emotionally, relationally, and spiritually. That last piece is the one that my buddy, Ski, wanted to help me handle. It's not like I'd never been to church. I learned about all that stuff when I was a kid. And, I remember trying to go with Kelly early on in our marriage. That's what you're supposed to do, right? It was the right image, and I *was* all about keeping up images.

We did go to a church. I remember walking in and being handed a program that would list off all the things that would be covered before I could get out of there to watch the game at home. I would open up the folded paper and begin checking things off as we went through the service. Some singing. Check. Some praying. Check. Say, "Good morning." Check. A reading or two. Check. Check. More singing. More praying. Check. Check. Maybe a personal story mixed in there. Check. A cracker and some grape juice. Check. Check. Take my money. Check. And tell me that I should go in peace and come back soon. I would and I would not. I knew that the minister would be walking back down the aisle soon, and I would be walking right after him. Then walking out the door. Running away. And, I wouldn't come back. Well, maybe I went back for an occasional Easter or Christmas. Now, I was just checking MY list to make sure I was doing exactly what I was "supposed" to do as somebody who believed in God.

When Ski invited me to come to RiverGlen Christian Church, I didn't expect much more than going through those same motions again. I went to church in February. I told Paul, "It's like Ben was talking to me! Sure, I have to get used to the modern music, but the message had me alert the entire time!"

I went back every week, and every week it felt like they were living in my house … in my HEAD! I began going to study groups and studying with Kelly, too.

My world had been turned upside down for so long. I'd turned my wife's world upside down. She could have turned so bitter, but she decided it was a blessing. I needed to fall before I could climb. I needed to lose before I could gain. Even our kids noticed how much we got into our new faith. It was the sole factor in bettering my and Kelly's relationship.

When you look at the story of Jonah in the Bible, he was running away from God, and I kind of see my own life the same way. Granted, there wasn't a big fish in my story. Still, I ran. I put myself first, and I put my family, and really anybody or anything else, last. When we came to that first service, I felt like the head pastor, Ben Davis, was talking right to me. Sitting in my chair that day, not just following a checklist before I could leave, was another one of those electric moments in my life, like the one I had experienced with my Carroll College football team almost twenty years earlier.

I was right where I was supposed to be.

Ben was talking about people who had strayed from their beliefs and weren't where they wanted to be in life as a result. I sure as heck wasn't where I wanted to be. He was talking about leading our families, which I needed to do before it was too late. So many people think that church and Christianity and God are about being good or doing good. That's not what it's about. It's about being changed. And, when you're changed, you can't help but do good.

I'll always remember Dad, my hard-working, tough-skinned, hands-off kind of father getting choked up when he shared with a friend, "That's when Bob's life changed. He would call us and start talking about RiverGlen. I could tell by his voice that his life had CHANGED. That's what got him where he is today."

Dad already knew, despite his quietness, what I was just learning. Real faith is about realizing that you are not the center of your own universe. When you become changed in your heart, good things just happen. You get good because of the change. You do good to continue that change in others, out of love, not obligation.

I was ready for the change. I don't know where it came from, but I started to cry that day in church. I pretended to have to wipe my glasses clean, but I knew right then that I was a fallen man and that Paul Paikowski's invitation was the greatest invitation of my life.

My wife and kids saw the difference in my heart. I asked them to come back every week. I even attended marriage conferences. Just like I went from being changed to saved, so did my marriage. Kelly and I learned that so much of what was in our lives was just stuff: unimportant material things … as IF I needed anything more in my life than the incredible blessings

I already had! I learned how to be there for my wife and my family, something I hadn't done … EVER.

Things had been falling apart for so long that it was hard to recognize when they began falling into place, but that's just what happened for this fallen man. I think of one of the basketball greats, Michael Jordan, when he said, "I've missed more than 9000 shots in my career. I've lost almost 300 games. 26 times, I've been trusted to take the game winning shot and missed. I've failed over and over and over again in my life. And that is why I succeed."

God was giving me the ball again despite all the shots I had missed. It's hard to describe just how drastically a man's life can be altered when he surrenders to a greater power. My finances were under control. We weren't rich, but we were managing. I saw my wife in a whole new light. I appreciated my children in a whole new way and began to change how I communicated with them. I used my work as a place where I could make a difference, not just in the streets, but in the hearts of those whose paths I crossed.

The biggest change of all was that I knew that I had value, even in low places and high pounds. I had worth. Even the other leaders in our church, like John Howard, the soft-spoken, energetic voice of RiverGlen's Men's Ministry, recognized the fast and drastic developments in me. He asked me to step up and help other men grow in their faith—ME!

I didn't need to be fixed, fit, or transformed to be worthwhile. I only needed to have an open heart and a willingness to make a better world.

I had purpose. I *HAVE* purpose.

Everybody's faith story is different, so it's hard to really share my journey without knowing that there are those who will hear it or read about it and roll their eyes. Nobody put their hands on me and pulled out evil spirits. Nobody shined a light down on me and sent a chorus to play in my heart. I wasn't whacked on the side of my head with a Bible. Hollywood loves to pretend that there is something wrong with people who believe in God. It's popular to make Christians look like prudes and Puritans or kooks and cultists. None of these are true.

Here is the proven, educated, experienced, undeniable, indisputable truth: belief in God—with your heart, your mind, your spirit, and (albeit, a little bit late for me) your body—is, more than anything, like falling in love for the first time. It is that feeling of such utter completeness that you're not sure how you were ever able to walk, or talk, or even breathe before you found it and lived for it. Except, completely unlike that nervousness that comes with love, or the fear that you could lose it, or the panic that you might screw it up, or the possibility of hurt or abandonment, you actually grow more stable and secure, and fuller with each passing day in His presence. FULL! Finally. After decades of constantly feeding my emptiness with society's servings, I was made *full*.

I had been shown so much grace that I was humbled completely, and I was completely … in love. I was broken down so that I could be built up better and stronger. Even though I was loved through all my mess-ups, I'm a bit of a slow learner. I spent almost two years in this zone of having new worth, a new heart, and a new life before I decided I wanted to make it permanent.

I had grown close with men from the church, including Pastor Ben, John Howard, and the tall, dark-haired, cool-handed, operational staff member, Steve Widmer. These men, who were kind, honest, smart, and sincere, were men I admired. And then there was Ski. I wouldn't have a

I met Paul Paikowski working narcotics with the Metropolitan Drug Unit in Waukesha County. He was the "religious guy" who pulled me away from the kind of life I was leading. Paul has been a friend and a mentor through both my spiritual transformation and then my physical transformation.

story to tell without Paul. There would have been no baptism. There would have been no *Extreme Weight Loss*. There might not have been a me.

I get told everyday how "great" I am. Paul didn't tell me I was great. He told me how great I could be. If I ever believed my own press, my head wouldn't fit through a door—Ski kept me together long enough to get my act together. I wanted to be a part of the brotherhood that made all of these men the loving, integrity-driven leaders they were.

November 13, 2010 was the best day of my life.

I chose to get baptized.

....

BEN SAYS:

> *"We didn't know if anybody would sign up. Bob was one of the few, and he ended up being one of the first to step out. We ended up baptizing 109 people that weekend! I think Bob helped with that. He has courage and steps out as a leader."*

JOHN SAYS:

> *"Bob set the example for his family. His wife is baptized now, too."*

STEVE SAYS:

> *"Bob was always a leader. It was always there, but now he's using it to lead people to good. He's committed to good.*

PAUL SAYS:

> *"The baptism was ceremonious. Bob was already there."*

....

Too often, in the Christian community, people abuse God's grace. Hypocrites are right up there with the Puritans and the kooks. Except more of them actually exist. Christians know that God accepts us as we are, so we don't try to be as good as we can for Him. We use His forgiveness as an excuse to live however we like because we know we are saved. Yet, His word also tells us:

- in 1 Corinthians that we must honor God with our bodies;
- in 1 Timothy that bodily training is of some value;
- in 3 John that being in good health goes well with your soul;
- in Romans that our bodies should be Holy and acceptable to God;
- in Hebrews that we must not be sluggish.

God tells us again and again that we must take care of ourselves, that we must not overindulge, including food, and that we must honor Him.

Why do we choose to ignore THESE verses?

(Why did I?)

Why do we choose to dishonor our God in THIS way?

(Why did I?)

These are just things dealing with our physical health. What about all of the things that being overweight and unhealthy also prevent us from doing to serve our greater purpose? Where would I find strength and energy to do what I was supposed to do at almost 450 pounds!

My pastor will be the first to explain how incredible the connection is between health and a person's spiritual life. God prepared us for good works. If a person's weight, energy, and health aren't good, he can't do what God called him to do.

It is TIME, as Christians, to make the commitment to confront this sin.

(It was that time for ME.)

I had a new purpose, and now, I needed a new body. Let's be honest. We're

Casting directors for Extreme Weight Loss *took my "mug shot" for the open casting call. I knew I was now on the right path.*

talking about addiction here. Addiction is really anything that is used as a replacement for God. For me, my commitment meant it was time to deal with nutrition and exercise, so I could begin to honor God with my body as His word tells us we must do.

I swallowed my pride.

I asked for help.

I remember picking up the devotional by Sarah Young, *Jesus Calling,* and a lesson stood out to me in one of the daily readings:

> *Leave outcomes up to Me. Follow Me wherever I lead, without worrying about how it will all turn out. [...] When our path leads to a cliff, be willing to climb it with My help.*

The new cliff I was led to ... the new climb ... was actually in front of the television. Ironic, I know. That's not usually the starting line for a healthy lifestyle. Kelly and I were watching the news one night, a channel that we never watch. God put me there at that time to show me the path I was supposed to take. Jeremiah 29:11 (NLT) says,

> *For I know the plans I have for you ... they are plans for good and not for disaster, to give you a future and a hope.*

I first worked out with John Pietenpol at Revolution Fitness in the summer of 2011, but I stopped exercising three months later and ended up gaining 100 pounds. After I was selected for Extreme Weight Loss, *he became my home-based trainer.*

Photo BTrick Photography

Holland Weathers, a casting director for *Extreme Weight Loss* was holding a casting call in Milwaukee for Season 3 of that show. I had known this woman from her time working in casting with *The Biggest Loser.* I didn't make those shows, obviously, but I always liked Holland, and she remembered me. Like so many associated with *Extreme Weight Loss,* her desire to help people was genuine. I clicked with her because of her sincerity, and she became a woman I would consider a lifelong friend.

As soon as I watched the news segment, I knew I was going that next day to the call. I had clarity, an epiphany. God had a plan for me. He had worked on my heart, and it was time for Him to work on my body. As He promised, He had plans for good to give me hope and a future. Everything seemed right. This was my purpose. This was what He intended me to do. For the first time in my adult life, I was pointing in the right direction, and it was in the direction of COMMITMENT, a word that would become the "C" in my new C.L.I.F., a God-honoring C.L.I.F.

I went back to the trainer I had worked with once before. John Pietenpol is the picture of health. He's this six-foot-something, blonde-haired, blue-eyed, tattooed but clean-cut guy in his mid-thirties. I had worked with him once before and told him that I needed to prove that I really was ready to make this change.

> *Merriam Webster—TRAINER: (noun) A staff member who trains athletes or gives first aid or therapy to injured players. See: John Pietenpol.*

This was a guy who looked like he belonged on the waves in California rather than shoveling the snow-covered walks in front of his Pewaukee, Wisconsin boutique gym, Revolution Fitness. Lucky for me, he could handle the cold. More than just being a great trainer, John wasn't going to let me slack off. He was tough. He played college in football, got a degree in Physical Education, married another fitness expert, and opened his business as a sort of dream. Now, he was going to become part of mine.

·························

Kelly along for the rollercoaster ride ...

"Bob promised me that, after trying out for The Biggest Loser *three times, he was done. My husband lied. He told me he was going to a football meeting, via a text message, when he was already gone to a casting call for* Extreme Weight Loss! *Four HOURS later, I texted 'WHERE ARE YOU?' He came home and told me he lied—he was at an open casting call for the show. Then, he told me he felt good about*

it, and I actually fell for his sales spiel.

I watch some reality TV, but I didn't really know how it would work. Extreme Weight Loss sent over a production team because they told us there was a chance we might be selected. They said they needed to do some test film of our family to see how we did. It's crazy. They come in at 7:30 in the morning, mic us up, and kind of take over. They marked out brand names and put all of these X's on my floor and my walls. I had to talk to the camera about Bob with these people I didn't know at all. It was nerve-wracking and emotional."

....

I admit there was a lot of pressure this time around. I went out for the show when my friends and family had been on so many roller coasters already. Kelly didn't want another letdown. Kayla wasn't on board with all these cameras taking over our personal lives. But, she had also said that I was disgusting. It hurts when that's how your own kids see you. She was seeing more than my obesity when she said those words, too. Jordan was rightfully skeptical because I'd tried out for other shows without success.

It was a very well-kept secret the day that I got chosen by Chris Powell to be one of his clients. My own big boss, the Waukesha County sheriff, pulled me over. Chris was with him to tell me I had been selected.

All of us were crying when Chris came to the car. We were overwhelmed with gratitude … and relief. This was actually going to happen. I was on my way to the California Health and Longevity Institute (CHLI).

....

CHLI was attached to the Four Seasons, and it was a plush, beautiful, spacious facility. I remembered seeing seasons one and two of *Extreme Weight Loss*, and walking into that huge entryway for the first time, I thought, "Wow! I've arrived. I'm here." (Cue the robotic voice in my head.)

I knew for me that this was a once-in-a-lifetime opportunity, and I felt it from that moment walking through the CHLI doors until my final weigh-in. It was like I had this dimmer switch that got turned on inside me when Chris gave me the news that I had been selected, and once in the foyer of the California Health and Longevity Institute, somebody had reached inside me and turned the switch up to full! It was like crossing that orange line onto my college football field, stepping into the station before a work shift, or, more important than ever before, crossing the threshold of the house to join the family I didn't deserve, all rolled into one.

I would spend hours in prayer, sitting on the edge of the beautiful fountain while I awaited interviews and other filming. With the new friends I would soon meet, Mike and Mehrbod, I would spend time in the spa, sweating off the pounds we didn't burn off at the gym.

My plan, once I got to CHLI, was to just keep an open mind and let the process happen. "God," I thought, "whatever you give me, you give me."

....

I was friends with Chris Powell right from the start! He and his wife Heidi, also an expert in transformations, don't do what they do—helping the morbidly obese get their health under control—for fame or fortune. Those things have come to them because they do what they do with Commitment, Love, Integrity, and Faith.

Please, God, let me work with them, I prayed.

The first time I saw Chris, this short-haired, solid man built like the compact, muscle-bound wrestlers of my high school days, it wasn't a wrestling singlet he was wearing; it was the neatly pleated, brown, tucked clothing of the Waukesha

Chris Powell not only chose me to be his client, but he also became my brother for life—Love ya, Buddy!

Sheriff's Department. He hid his smiling face in the shadow of a brimmed police officer's hat and the glimmering promise in his eyes behind a pair of mirrored lenses fit for Eric Estrada in his *CHIPS* days.

Please, God, let me work with them, I prayed.

Heidi Powell is a pretty huge part of Chris's team, too, and not just in keeping their four children organized and cared for but also in the transformation process. Heidi is a beautiful, long-haired pixie of a woman—as tiny as the little blonde Tinkerbell and as powerful as the iron pots that fairy would shape—whose huge, contagious smile and anime eyes are only trumped by the size of her heart. I would get to know the Powell family over the next year and come to see them as part of my family. Chris would be my confidant, my physical engine, and my fitness motivator. Heidi was an ear to me and to Kelly as we navigated the emotional and spiritual side of the changes that would take place.

Please, God, let me work with them, I prayed.

I prayed at CHLI like I'd never prayed before in my life. I prayed that I could get the help I needed. I prayed that it wasn't too late. I prayed that I was healthy enough to get healthier still. I prayed that this would be the final piece to making me the husband Kelly deserved. I prayed and prayed and prayed and prayed.

Just like the coaches of my twenties helped me to climb, the cavalry-like partners of my thirties kept me alive despite falling, and the courageous, Christian leaders of my forties picked me back up, God had put these incredible people in my path to help me continue on it toward being a better man. When Chris told me that he was going to help me become healthy, he was really telling me,

Hey! I'm here in answer to a prayer.

By the end of our year together, he'd add *"Buddy!"* to that.

CHRIS SAYS:

"I wasn't in this for 365 days. I'm in it for a lifetime."

I had worked with John Pietenpol once before Extreme Weight Loss, *and he helped me most with the physical part of my transformation. He was tough and wouldn't let me slack off. I still work out at John's gym.*

Chris helped me most with the psychological transformation. We are still good friends.

Chris and Heidi sincerely love the clients who become cast members of their show. LOVE! They get that most of us don't have love for ourselves at the time that we submit to them, so they just give us that much more to help make up the difference.

HEIDI SAYS

> "I think for Chris, Bob became a friend early on after the surprise. I remember him coming back and having so many stories about Bob, bonding and talking. He got to wear a cop uniform, which he loved, and I remember him coming back and saying, 'You know what? He's somebody I would be friends with outside of the show.' I think the connection was almost immediate for Chris. Every communication they had, he'd pass along to me."

It's hard to portray people who are known from their small-screen appearances to the world because we live in such a skeptical time, but Chris and Heidi are about as genuine as they come. I remember when one of my colleagues first met them in person, she was blown away by how truly kind they both were. They exude joy. They give their time and their energy out of the goodness of their hearts. They are always positive. The only thing Chris and Heidi have in greater supply than their graciousness are the life stories they have inspired and motivated to healthful success.

Chris and Heidi Powell know that transformation is not about just dropping pounds. I'd done that before, with all my crash diets. Transformation needed to be something bigger for a man who was bigger than most. Transformation starts on the inside in order to fix what the world sees on the outside.

HEIDI SAYS

> "He came to us ready. He came to the table with what he needed to break through. Chris and I didn't talk about this, but the difference between Bob's transformation and a lot of others is that Bob made God the center of his transformation. The process of loving himself? His focus was really on loving God. That was his commitment."

I was committed to this change. The Powells were committed to helping me. Now, I needed to see if the show was committed to keeping me around. I called Kelly and told her that I was ready. I was doing this whether or not I made the show.

Being selected meant that I got the chance to basically compete with another 35 to 40 individuals who were all in the same, desperate, obese need for one of the thirteen cast member slots that would have the honor and opportunity. I met Mike Epstein and Mehrbod Mohammadi, and we became immediate friends. We were The Three Amigos.

Mike would do just about anything to get a guy to smile. What he offered was friendship and his love of (and inspiration from) superheroes. He wanted all of us to be superheroes, too. At 49 years old, the Jewish family man was the oldest cast member the show had ever worked with. He never let it stop him. When I broke a record for largest percentage of weight lost on the show's history, Mike worked on his own goal of lowest body fat percentage.

To round out our little trio was Mehrbod Mohammadi. Mehrbod was and is one of the most loving souls I've ever known. Everybody who meets him, loves him. He is so good to everybody! He idolizes his grandfather and cherishes his parents, and he is a good brother, good fiancée, and an all-around good guy. He was just so witty that he could pop out with all sorts of funny quips. He was spontaneous and smart, and I am happy to count him among my lifelong friends.

So, a Christian, a Jew, and an Arab walk into CHLI together and become a great accountability team for one another. Now, if we could just make it through the initial medical tests, lessons, talks, production interviews, weigh-ins, workouts, and screen time, that would determine whether we could be one of the thirteen lucky people with the honor to work beside Chris Powell for a full year during our transformations.

Not everybody makes it through to final selection. I remember one great guy who was a little harsh at first—kind of an "Ole Boys Club" sort of man. He was full of old-fashioned sexism on the surface, but if you could get him alone when the cameras weren't rolling, he'd warm up and pull out pictures of the wife and daughter, who he really loved … who he wanted to continue loving for a lot longer than doctors told him he'd have. The boisterous guy was just an act.

He didn't make the show. The strain that we were going to put on our bodies over the next year would be too much for some. I really liked this guy! When I was back at CHLI at my nine-month mark for skin removal surgery, he visited us and was in even worse shape. When we waved goodbye, I had a daunting feeling that it would be my final *"Bye, Buddy,"* to him. He passed away before the season finished taping.

MORBID obesity is not just some random phrase. Morbid means having to do with death. FAT to the point of DYING! That is what all the people at Finals Week were. This *was* life or death, and I prayed for life.

Chris and Heidi later told me that, in those initial talks, they look for reactions from people to know that we're truly getting it. They don't just want people who are nodding along and giving the sort of trained right response, but they want to know that we're going to practice what we're being taught as opposed to just putting on a show for them.

CHRIS SAYS

> *"Because cop and coach was Bob for so long, as the saying goes, it's hard to teach an old dog new tricks. The whole time I was thinking that he had lived that for so long, would he even be open to exploring something outside of that and thinking of who he really might be? What if he's not just Bob the football coach or Bob the police officer? Who is he? Through and through, I was like, 'this guy is so stuck in his rut; I don't know if I can get him out.'"*

Looking around the room, I saw a group of the most charismatic men and women I'd ever met in my life. There was every age, race, gender, and background; these were a lot of really talented individuals. ALL of them were there because they wanted to change and save their lives. Who was I that I deserved this opportunity over them. I didn't feel like I had a choice but to fight though. I was having my own *It's a Wonderful Life* moment, praying with all my heart, *"I WANT TO LIVE."* I had to awaken my inner Jimmy Stewart!

We spent a lot of time in that room, waiting, waiting. You would look at others and start comparing yourself in your head. The tension would build which, by the way, isn't recommended for a room full of potential heart attacks. We were lucky to have a great crew of off-camera leaders who kept our minds occupied.

I'll never forget when producer, Matt Assmus, came into the room and saw all of us sitting in there settled somewhere between bored and anxious. Matt is a small-framed man who is always moving. Even when he's standing still, you can watch his eyes and you know that he is picturing the next dozen shots … lighting, sound, camera angles, placement of people … all of it! I can't help but conjure up images of a sound producer with a huge soundboard that he operates like an instrument, except Matt's board is in his mind, and we were all the knobs and dials. It was a privilege to be able to watch Matt work.

Everything had been so tense with producers always telling you something in your ear. There was a lot of strutting going on, and we stood the chance of becoming rivals rather than allies. That's not what this show was about. We needed to lighten things up. Matt looked around the room with conference tables against the walls and a large empty space down the middle. "Hey!" he called out, kind of off the cuff, "Who's going to take me on in a push up challenge?"

There were no cameras. This was just Matt loosening up all of us. We weren't even sure he was serious at first, until he made his way to the clear space.

"I'll do it," I said, and I took my shirt off of my 448-pound body in front of everybody. It was nice not to have to be self-conscious in this room full of a whole lot of folks who were in the same boat as I was.

MEHRBOD SAYS:

> *"The first experience I had with Bob was during my second day at camp for* Extreme Weight Loss. *He was asked if he could do pushups, and he immediately got down and did 10 pushups without breaking a sweat. I was blown away. He wasn't faking it. This wasn't pushups on his knees, which I couldn't do even if I tried!"*

Actually, I only did five, and I was sweating profusely!

I wouldn't want to have to determine who is and isn't sincere. I only knew that I needed this. I also knew I was in a new mission field, committed to good. I wasn't a rival to these other finalists. I was their brother. I understood what they felt, and they understood me. I decided to try to help people out. I knew that we would all be better people if we were in better health. I genuinely wanted everybody to succeed.

HEIDI SAYS:

> *"Besides his physical stature, one thing about Bob is that he was a leader. I remember people watching everything he did and trying to emulate him as the example. This was huge to me. I realized that this was somebody who can pull people to him, and they were going to come to him regardless, but he was going to take them and help them. He gave them the pats on the back, the lifting up that they needed. He lived everything we said and taught and really helped us rally the troops and motivate and inspire."*

Chris actually told me that he appreciated my background in coaching and police work. He thought coaching helped me to lead, and my police work helped with some of the psychological parts of the process.

CHRIS SAYS:

> *"He didn't just preach it. Everybody preached it, but he would lead by example. He would offer assistance and guidance and he never forced, just helped. That's where I truly believe his background in working with others—even the training from police work helped. People need to want this. In order to really motivate and inspire, though, you need to lead others by example."*

There's an expression based on Timothy 3:16–17 (NLT) in the Bible that says,

> *God doesn't call the equipped, He equips the called.*

Once again, I was given a new brotherhood. From brother, to team, to the brotherhood of police officers, to my Christian brotherhood, and finally, to the incredible members of my *Extreme Weight Loss* accountability team headed up by my new brother, Chris. Again and again, I was able to look back on my life and see the lessons and preparation I was given to last through each transition and transformation I would have to face. I went out to Finals Week with the intention of remaining committed. I was blessed with a commitment from *Extreme Weight Loss* to see me through my weight loss transformation. Here I was, once again, right where I needed to be …

 … *committed.*

At the start of my weight transformation, I got to go onto a loading dock. This is where a guy my size gets weighed. It's no small embarrassment to be measured by the same equipment used to carry entire pallets of goods. There was nothing good about the number I got while standing there with Chris Powell and a television crew: 448 pounds. I would have to lose more than half of that to become a healthy man.

Transformation: Sweet!

There are three categories of processes responsible for your metabolic burn. 60 to 70 percent of the calories you burn in a given day are burnt just by being alive. [...] Another 10 to 15 percent is accomplished by the simple act of digesting your food [...]. That last 15 to 30 percent comes from physical activity [...]. All that said, a balanced diet is extremely important to keeping healthy, and again—if you want to shed fat, keep the calories coming in lower than the calories you burn.

~The Science of Fat
by: Brent Rose

Transformation *is* SWEET! The way the pounds melt off in the beginning, the clothes that you get rid of, knowing you'll never have to wear them again, and—oh yeah—the whole *not* being afraid you might die thing doesn't suck either. All the weight loss milestones, from seeing my own feet (and other body parts) again, to not being afraid to see my own reflection are definite rewards and natural highs. Choosing to keep those highs going is a no-brainer: *"Piece of cake!"*

That being said, as a food addict, I absolutely still craved (and crave) that literal piece of cake from time to time. There is an anonymous quotation that says, "Mourning your abstinence from junk food is like mourning the loss of an enemy who would happily see you die." It is not just important, but vital, that nutrition is a part of an obese person's short- and long-term plan for recovery. When I called Kelly from Finals Week to tell her the transformation was going to happen with or without *Extreme Weight Loss,* I told her we needed to get rid of the crap food in our house ... all of it.

I was lucky to have Chris Powell's team get me going on a basic nutrition plan:

- **Tuesday through Sunday, I would consume:**
  - **5 Meals per Day**
  - **1800 Calories per Day**
  - **1/2 of my Body Weight in Ounces of Water per Day (A 150-pound person should drink 75 oz. of water per day. I would start out drinking 224 oz. per day.)**
- **Monday was my Flex Day:**
  - **Bump Up Calories 40%**
  - **Allow Myself a Treat**

I chose Mondays as my flex days because weekends had been weak days in the past. It would be bad for me to let my guard down while surrounded by a dozen ways to compromise my nutrition when I needed just a simple easing of the tension. It didn't matter what day I chose, as long as I had a time that would feel like a reward and not make me fall too far from my plan.

Once a week, though, I would have this day to look forward to. On flex days, I would opt to get my extra calories from something that wouldn't stop me in my tracks. I wanted something that calorically satisfied while still providing nutrients. For me, that meant a burger with cheddar cheese in a lettuce wrap. My treat on flex days would be a serving of frozen yogurt.

As a food addict, of course, I also had in place some tips and tricks for dealing with the cravings. The cravings come and, if ignored, they can turn from craving to binge. Some of my favorite craving treatments include:

- A 12 oz. Glass of Water
- A Serving-Size (7 to 12 Counted Out) of Almonds
- Saving Your Cravings for Your Flex Day

John Pietenpol remained my trainer when I was in Wisconsin during my weight loss. He also provided a few tips.

As part of the new eating plan, the idea was to stick with my calories and water intake, eat foods that satisfy nutritionally as well as calorically, and have a plan for when cravings attack. Many people have asked about that great "diet food." I don't like the word "DIET" anymore. Nothing in my nutritional transformation was about diet. A person's approach to eating needs to be lifestyle. Setting that aside, I do have one food that I swapped out and added to my refrigerator: bulk Greek yogurt.

- 12 to 14 Grams of Protein
- A Longer-Lasting "Full" Sensation than Traditional yogurts (Which are Mostly Sugar)
- The Body Works Longer to Break it Down
- The Thicker Consistency Helps Fool the Brain

When I came into this weight transformation, I was recovering from bankruptcy and, at the same time, taking unpaid time off work to be at the California Health and Longevity Institute. I GET that eating healthy can seem like an expensive option in a society with discount and dollar menus (full of deep fried fat) at every major intersection. Eating right does not have to be eating expensively.

- Shop at the Discount Grocery Store (Put Aside Your Pride for this One!)
- Buy your Staples in Bulk
- Chicken Thighs Cost Less Than Chicken Breasts (Remove the Skin to Keep it Healthy)
- Apples and Bananas are Reasonably Priced Fruits
- Shop the Season and the Sales

At the start of the day, every day, I had to decide I would make good decisions throughout the day, so that, at the end of the day, I could call it … a good day.

- **Do Not Have Junk in Your House ... PERIOD**
- **Eat More Meals with Fewer Calories**
- **High Water Intake**
- **EAT Nutrient-Fulfilling Foods**
- **DEVISE Pre-determined Solutions for Cravings**
- **Set Aside Times for Reasonable Flexibility**
- **Shop Discounts, Seasons, and Sales**

These tips are part of how I made my transformation ...
... *sweet.*

Being L.oved

But anyone who does not love does not know God, for God is love.

~1 John 4:8 (NLT)

Up until this point in my life, all of my "love chapters" were about *me*. Man, was I messing up. God's love chapter says, in Philippians 1:9-11 (NLT),

> *I pray that your love will overflow more and more, and that you will keep on growing in knowledge and understanding. For I want you to understand what really matters, so that you may live pure and blameless lives until the day of Christ's return. May you always be filled with the fruit of your salvation—the righteous character produced in your life by Jesus Christ—for this will bring much glory and praise to God.*

I was the luckiest guy on the planet when I was selected to work with the *Extreme Weight Loss* team to lose my pounds. I was shown such incredible love during that time. However, while all this was going on, my greatest love was about to lose something, too, or, maybe, gain something. Kelly was and is my best friend, my confidant, my supporter, and my heart. And, with a heart big enough to love me at my biggest, she was bound to share that love with people other than me. This was going to be a year of transformation through love for so many people.

Kelly has a brother and sister and, in her words, her sister, Heather, got the short end of the stick. Heather has polycystic kidney disease (PKD). It comes in two unwelcome forms. Sometimes, it's detected in utero. Often, those children don't live past two or three years old before dying of kidney failure due to persistent cysts that build up on the kidneys. Heather got the sneakier, quieter version. An adult with PKD can spend years before they even know they're sick. Once an adult is sick, they're on a timeline.

They get tired.

They get weak.

They get ill.

They get dialysis.

Eventually, and if they're lucky, they get a new kidney so that they can get a new chance at life.

PKD was detected in Heather when she was in her early thirties. That's the typical age that the disease is discovered in adults. We learned that the disease was hereditary after Heather's diagnosis, and it turned out that both Kelly's mother and her brother had polycystic kidney disease as well. Nobody knows how quickly it will progress. You could live your whole life without progression, or it hits you hard and fast. Kelly's brother was diagnosed when her sister was already in bad shape. She never had to push Kelly. Kelly told her she could have her kidney. Our kids were old enough, and so they understood. I had inquired about being tested for Heather too, but I was morbidly obese at the time. It wasn't an option.

Kelly's mom got a transplant from a non-family member who matched. That didn't leave a whole lot of options for Heather. Her brother was still doing fine. Kelly was approved as Heather's kidney donor in April 2012, just one month before I got picked up for *Extreme Weight Loss*.

I was home for a few days, which was when Kelly had her transplant. Then, the film crew was here when she was less than two weeks post-op. She went from being healthy to sick while her sister went from being sick to healthy ... but, in the long-run, both are okay. Kelly even ended up joining my weight loss journey even though she couldn't start really working out until after my skin removal surgery at the nine-month mark.

In the middle of my incredible transformation, I was surrounded by people cheering me on. Meanwhile, my wife was transforming lives of her own ... the humble heroine. Kelly was in the business of saving lives and sharing love. I was being given a great gift of love with the show. I was also given a great supporter who loved me. How, in the middle of this realization, could I do anything other than learn to love myself?

CHRIS SAYS

> *"Transformation is not the process of losing weight, it's the journey toward loving yourself, and as soon as he learned that lesson and learned the steps toward loving himself and loving others, that's when HE transformed."*

I discovered that the only straight path back to loving myself was to accept love from others. From God amd my church, from family, and from a huge community of health and fitness supporters ... I was blanketed in love. I always had been really, but I finally opened my eyes to see it.

Kelly supported me in the home, clearing out the foods that I couldn't have around and even giving up one of her own favorite hobbies of baking. She supported me in the faith journey that we took together. She supported me by working out with me even when it was as hard for her due to her kidney donation as it was for me due to my bum knees.

That word "LOVE" has gotten so diluted in our society. It's not just the phrase, *"Love ya!"* between people who barely know each other, it's that same exchange used just as often in fan worship. It's how we LOVE certain shows and LOVE certain foods and LOVE certain sports or hobbies. In a world where *love* is everywhere, it's hard to recognize it anywhere.

So, let me dispense with all the mush and tell you something that is not a very traditional love story. While on *Extreme Weight Loss*, one of the great blessings I had was the opportunity to visit Paris where I would get the chance to bike two of the same routes that are used for the *Tour de France.* (A few bragging rights here, too. I kicked Chris's tail on these race legs! Ever the perfect trainer, he told me that it was one of his proudest moments—when the student surpasses the teacher.)

CHRIS SAYS

> *"There is a saying—something about finding so much joy when the people you teach can take everything you've done and shown and bring it to a whole new level. Then, you've really done your job."*

We went to France with all the stereotypes in place. It's dirty. People are rude. They hate Americans. I'm happy to say that none of these clichés were true. Paris was a wonderful city.

What I didn't expect, though, was that Paris had another unexpected, but very noticeable problem. There are a whole lot of little dogs in the city and no little "pick up after your dog" rules in Paris. Not to get too graphic, but the city was covered in more than its share of dog droppings. As an American tourist

During our bike ride in France, Chris and I had to take an espresso and bathroom break in a quaint town.

in Paris, I never quite got the hang of watching every single step I took, and my shoes suffered the consequences.

The cameras weren't rolling. It was cold and wet outside. The rain had been coming down for most of the day. Chris Powell and I were tired and, sure enough, I stepped in it. Chris reached up to a tree and grabbed a small branch that was hanging. He pulled it off, asked for my shoe, and cleaned it with the leaves. Then he ran the sole of the shoe back and forth in the storm water that was running like a stream along the side of the street. He wasn't above the menial task of cleaning up dog crap. I asked him about it later and he said, "No problem, Buddy. I got your back … and your shoe."

I knew he meant it. Chris was the guy who was there, pushing me through when my knee popped out, when I'd messed up my ACL, my meniscus, and any other part of the knee you could find on an X-ray, first on one knee, then the other. Chris was the guy who awakened my inner athlete to push me beyond physical discomfort. He hopped in the pool with me and biked through the bitter cold rain. Chris and I became great friends who really care about each other. He's my brother.

Our friendship didn't end when the cameras stopped rolling. We call to check up on each other and our families for holidays, special occasions, or no occasion at all.

HEIDI SAYS

> *"I remember one time when Bob called and I started to offer him encouragement. I wanted to see how he was doing. In reality, he had called to check up on us. Bob always did things like that. His relationship with us wasn't about what he could get from us."*

Sometimes, to help you build that love for yourself, you need to see it in others. Then, you need to show it to others. I wasn't used to doing that. American relationship researcher, Barbara De Angelis said: "If you aren't good at loving yourself, you will have a difficult time loving anyone, since you'll resent the time and energy you give another person that you aren't even giving to yourself." I wasn't used to loving myself, much less any good at it. I wasn't used to loving others. I wasn't used to feeling love from others. When you have somebody who cares about you, such as a parent, a mentor, a spouse, or kids, they're usually around for you, even when you screw up and make bad decisions, and when you're ready to make things right.

I got a second glimpse of love in France, too. It was a second glimpse of the person who had been there for me through it all, willing to love me when I couldn't love myself, and being my emotional bank when every bank of my own was completely withdrawn. While in France, Kelly and I celebrated our twentieth anniversary. I had given her diamond earrings, but, truly, she outdid me.

We had already received so many blessings that she wanted to give me a gift from her heart. Her words, from a letter that she read to me in person while in Paris, were one of the pieces of armor forged by love that would help to keep me strong and protected through the rest of my weight loss transformation.

> *"… nothing I could buy would be able to symbolize how proud I am of you and the man you are becoming. Our journey has not always been smooth, but we are on such a solid path. I knew I couldn't change you (you know I tried) until you decided that you needed to work on yourself emotionally and physically. I am so incredibly grateful for you and your transformation. I am a blessed woman to be able to share life's journey with you. I love you … ."*

I was in the heart of a great *C.ommitment* and had great *L.ove* in my heart.

I was at the base of a new C.L.I.F.

•••••••••••••••••••••••••

People don't always believe me when I tell them that my transformation wasn't about the weight loss so much as what I could do once the weight *was* lost. One guy who got it was my kid brother, Bruce. He was such a great supporter!

BRUCE SAYS

> *"At no time did I think he wouldn't make his goal. I knew how badly he wanted it. Once an athlete, always an athlete. Bob just needed the guidance. He needed the know-how. Once he was chosen, it clicked for him the very first day. I met Chris Powell and told him, 'Thanks, Chris. Thanks for choosing my brother and giving him another chance to live.' He told me he didn't do anything. He was just there, and Bob made the commitment."*

I think when this all happened, it made us closer. We started talking more and more because Bruce was into the running thing. He would always call and ask me, "What did you do today? How was your workout?" He was always positive and encouraging.

I remember telling Bruce when my knees quit on me that I was still going to follow through. "I'm still doing it," I told him. "I may actually have to swim."

For every pound of weight on your body, your knees feel three pounds of pressure. So imagine what it was like for knees that had already been surgically repaired once before to be lugging pressure equivalent to almost 1400 pounds. When my knees quit, I could have quit too, and most people would have been okay with it. Instead, I went to the pool at Westwood Health and Fitness. The people there were fit and had been swimming their whole lives. Me? I put on my triple extra large swim trunks, surrounded by people half my age and a quarter of my size. I don't know what they were thinking or seeing. I had to decide if I was more committed to being self-conscious or to being a new self. Bruce was one of the guys who wanted me, more than anything, to succeed and to share those workouts together.

BRUCE SAYS:

> *"Now, I have my big brother back and somebody I can do triathlons with. We ended up doing Tri-Rock in Lake Geneva, Wisconsin. We were talking about it. I had never done a triathlon before, and we decided to do it together.*

I needed to train because I was only a runner, but he was working out and swimming. It was September 15, 2012. It was so neat. You know, it was finally something that I could do with my brother besides fishing. It was finally a sporting event we could share. I wasn't the junior varsity guy or Peewee league when he was older. It's not football. It's not wrestling. We were together.

Bob even beat me in the swim, and I told him, 'I won't cross the finish line without you.' In the first transition, between swimming and biking, I said to Bob, 'let's go.' I was in it for the time. He was in it for the experience. We got on the bike together but lost each other on the course. I ended up finishing, but I went back to get my brother. 'Dude, we gotta finish strong,' I told him. The athlete in him started booking it. I told him we would finish together.

I had my hand on his shoulder, and we crossed together. In my family, you didn't hear a lot of, 'I love you,' but I got to say, 'I'm proud of you.' It's something I never said to him, but this was a brand new Bob."

Kelly's Letter

Robert,

There really isn't much I can do to surprise you or to top you giving me diamond earrings at the Eiffel Tower, but what I can give you is my heart. I made a promise to you 20 years ago not knowing what the next days or years would bring and, looking back, there were times I wanted to break that promise.

We have been blessed with good health and two beautiful kids, but we've also endured terrible times in our marriage and financial failure. Not so many years ago, I was done. At least, that's what I told myself. But, for some reason, I couldn't let go. I never really knew why. Lord knows people were telling me to, but I just couldn't.

Now I know. Even in the midst of our troubled times, I knew there was at the core of you, a good and decent man, a man whose morals and values, though sometimes skewed, were, at the core, good and true. Trying to get you to listen to those morals and values was a different story.

I thank God everyday that you opened your heart to a conversation that included HIM. Without you making a conscious decision to explore your faith, I'm not sure where we would be today. I let you lead the way in our faith journey, knowing that is your way: leading. I am humbled and in awe of how much you have grown as a man and as a husband.

This faith journey led you to a decision that has changed both of our lives and our family's as well. Your weight loss struggle could not be conquered on your own. Your heart had to be right, and once that was good, you had to do something extreme—I just had no idea HOW extreme!

When Chris shocked us by choosing you, I was beyond words! I was so excited, happy for you because you were becoming a new man on the inside, and I wanted you to be able to be a new man on the outside as well. You see, your total transformation started well before that day, but Chris was going to help you finish it.

Six months in and I'm amazed and awed again and again by your drive and dedication. I know your knees remind you every moment of every day how easy and understandable it would be for you to give up. You can barely walk. Somehow, you find the inner fortitude to push past the pain. This process has seen you try experiences you never dreamed of! Your knees opened the door to kayaking. When you told me that, all I could do was smile! I thought about us whitewater rafting with the kids years ago and how they almost couldn't find a life jacket that would fit you. Now, you're kayaking around lakes and rivers and swimming across other lakes (literally) to raise money for the Wounded Warrior Project.

I know you would love to play basketball, but your knees won't allow you to. If your knees were good, you would never have taken up cycling. I

Photo courtesy of Andy Drefs

Kelly's letter didn't make the final cut of my Extreme Weight Loss episode, but sharing her sentiments on national TV was the most touching, loving moment of my transformation.

know you loved riding your motorcycle before you gave it up, but now you get the same sense of calm coming home after a monster bike ride. 20 years ago, if you would've told me you'd go to a yoga class, let alone "hot yoga," I would've had a heart attack. The fact that you go on football Sundays is a testament to what has become important to you.

You and I seem to do our best communicating through the written word. Nothing I could buy would be able to symbolize how proud I am of you and the man you are becoming. Our journey has not always been smooth, but we are on such a solid path. I knew I couldn't change you (you know I tried) until you decided that you needed to work on yourself emotionally and physically. I am incredibly grateful for you and your transformation.

I am a blessed woman to be able to share life's journey with you. I love you. My heart is and always will be yours.

Love,
Me

Transformation: Sweat!

The good news about sweating and weight loss is that sweating is usually a result of the body trying to rid itself of excessive heat produced by the cells doing work, and work burns calories. In other words, it is the loss of calories from exercise that is the useful withdrawal from our calorie account that matters not the sweat itself."

~Weight Loss and Sweating it Off
by: Mike Hirn

Transformation *means* SWEAT! I was going to have to work. As motivational speaker, Steve Pavlina puts it, "When you live for a strong purpose, then hard work isn't an option. It's a necessity." It was going to suck. I had a home gym put in by *Extreme Weight Loss*, but I was done hiding what I'd become to prevent me from becoming someone better. This time, when I sweat, it wasn't going to be with somebody handing over a paper towel and looking at me with pity. It was going to be with somebody handing over a water bottle and looking at me with pride. John Pietenpol was every bit as much a part of the fitness piece of my weight loss as Chris Powell. Revolution Fitness was my second home for six days a week, several hours a day, and it is still my gym today.

The hard thing about attacking weight loss, when you need to do so much of it, is that you need to start out small. You won't be able to exercise the same way as a person who is already in shape simply because you have so much mass to move around a heart, lungs, and arteries that are weak and fragile.

As I got started, I needed to set achievable fitness goals and be very aware of my body in a different way than I had before. I needed to stop loathing it and start listening to it.

- **Monitor Effort and Exhaustion Levels**
- **Consider Heart Rate Monitors**
- **Start Low Impact While Still Heavy**
- **Be Willing to Change as Weight Changes**

I was also lucky to work with John as he agreed with Chris about the need to change things up and be flexible. If a body gets too used to the same routine, it doesn't react in the same way.

John was always changing things for me; his other clients and I really credit his approach with helping me achieve the results I did. Circuits are doing a few different exercises, one after another, and then repeating that "circuit" two or three times. Sometimes, those circuits, his "cardio-circuits," were all about getting that heart rate going and really burning those calories. Tabata is this newer approach to fitness that involves bursts of going all out on an exercise for 20 seconds and stopping for 10 seconds, or doubling those times on a Friday-40 day. Then, he had his Revometrix days where he would combine two exercises for cardio and abs and two for strength and abs. You'd do those combined exercises back to back in sort of mini-circuits. Then, every once in a while, the Saturday curveball would land on something that you really love and that worked for you. And, even though Revolution Fitness was closed on Sundays, I worked out every day during my transformation—seven days a week, three hours a day. The point was not WHAT I did. The point was that I did SOMETHING.

No excuses.

My knees were another issue—as was chronicled in my *Extreme Weight Loss* episode. They had been bad most of my life. I used to tell people they got that way from sports. That wasn't untrue, but I'm sure lugging around more than double the amount of weight they were made for didn't do them any good either. That's when I had to take to the pool.

No excuses.

- **Change Up Your Exercise Routine**
- **Give Your All to EVERY Workout**
- **No Excuses**

Once again, God had put people in my path to help me on that path. John Pietenpol was such an incredible asset. Unfortunately, because of his abilities, there are those who think they can't achieve their weight loss without the people or the professional equipment. There are always answers to this problem. If you can't afford a gym membership or a home gym:

- **Do Hill Repeats at a Local Park**
- **Pick Up a Used Bike and Hit the Trails**
- **Use the Internet to Find Free Training Videos**
- **Get DVDs from the Library**
- **Many Insurance Programs Help with Gym Costs**
- **There is Financial Assistance Available from Some Gyms and Pools**
- **Ask for Help!!!**

A person can also choose to work out right in the home. You can get DVDs from the library. Basic, functional movement exercises include:

- **Sit-ups**
- **Push-ups**
- **Mountain Climbers**
- **Burpees**
- **Planks**
- **Ab Workouts on a Gym Ball**

More importantly, where are you putting your money?
What's your priority?
Do you have skin in the game?

You have to want to do it. If it's a priority, you will accomplish it. I would love to travel around the world, but I have CHOSEN to put my finances into two major areas: my kids' education and my health. I choose not to put my money into travel, the bar, alcohol, or going out to eat. I have taken money from those other areas that weren't positive in my own life and put that money into those areas that make me better.

Make the choice to make exercise work.

- **Start According to Your Abilities**
- **Be Flexible**
- **Change Up Your Routine**
- **Use the Resources Available to You**
- **Work Out at Home**
- **Make Fitness a Priority**
- **ACCEPT NO EXCUSES**

With good, sweating tips, a person's transformation is …
… *no sweat.*

I.ntegrity in Everything

The Lord detests lying lips, but he delights in those who tell the truth.

~Proverbs 12:22 (NLT)

God tells us in 1 Samuel 2:30 that *"… He will honor those who Honor Him."* We don't deny this when it comes to the most obvious of sins: drinking until drunk, adultery, anger, and theft. We know that these dishonor God. But, we forget that, in His eyes, all sin is equal. God also puts us where we need to be to make a change for good. Throughout my life, He put people in my path to help me and courageously set me straight. Now, I was being put into people's paths. I needed to stay on my path. Obviously, the path started at the gym. Being true to my workouts and pouring myself all the way into every one of them, every time, was important. It's what people saw, but this was different from the image I had wanted people to see. This time, I wanted them to see a CHANGE.

CHRIS SAYS:
> *"He's a coach, but as a good coach should be, he's coachable. That's what makes him different."*

I remember at the beginning of my time with *Extreme Weight Loss* when Chris Powell talked to his future, potential clients during Finals Week. When he talked about integrity, I thought about how hard I worked at my job. I was trustworthy, loyal, and hard-working. When it came to my family, I knew I had never strayed, and I brought in financial provisions.

Then, Chris said, "I'm not talking about that. I'm talking about keeping promises to yourself."

I needed to learn to not just honor my own integrity in fitness and nutrition but in everything else, too. I had made promises to myself, my loved ones, and my God that I would get healthy, and my personal integrity needed to be intact. I needed to keep those promises.

CHRIS SAYS:

> "When you're on a weight loss journey, you trade addictions. With food, you get an immediate payout. There's the flavor, and the textures, and the sensation of fullness. There's that payout. When they trade to exercise, you get the numbers on the scale every week. People play the numbers game. When people go in for surgery, you get laid out for 6 weeks, you don't get that numbers payout. Bob wasn't playing the numbers game. He was prepared for that, and as nice as that payout was, his numbers were great— his body was physically addicted to the exercise. BUT, his payout was integrity. His 'feel good' was about keeping promises and fulfilling commitments. Instead of looking at the number on the scale, he would look at the end goal, the purpose. That's how he would get his payout is through follow through, and that's what kept him feeling good. As long as he chased that carrot, it would always get him where he needed to be. As long as you are chasing the integrity carrot, that's the best addiction there is in the world."

Integrity is something I learned when I had to dig deep to push through a workout or a food temptation, or drive past a fast food restaurant. The hardest thing about that year was what I would do when nobody was watching. But, you can't hide the fact that you're cheating on fitness or nutrition. It literally shows on your body. And, as a Christian, I know that God is always watching. Other people were watching me, too.

JOHN HOWARD SAYS:

> *"Since Bob's transformation, one of the things he has now is credibility. We hear about life coaches out there smoking, drinking, and eating crap. He's real. Bob gives credibility to the fact that you can CHANGE no matter where you are. There are groups dealing with addictions, and certainly food addiction, and he's a leader they can trust."*

Because I was on display every week before so many different groups—my family, my department, my church, and my gym—I had built-in accountability. This was integrity. Keeping up my change for myself was integrity, too. I wouldn't make my new C.L.I.F. climb without truth in my heart.

Despite the fact that I was losing the weight and getting fit, I did not make my six-month goal. I missed it by 8 pounds. I was crushed. My knees were a mess, so I had to back off some of the higher impact workouts, but I was so disappointed in my intensity level that I pushed myself even more after that. That caused even more damage. My accountability took a different form when that happened. In order to be able to pick up the intensity, I would have to have my knees repaired even if it took me out of the game for a while. I had to concentrate on nutrition alone.

Having Chris, The Three Amigos, other cast members, and, of course, my family, is what really helped me through that time. An addict is an addict. I had been able to fill so much of my daily time with workouts, so I wasn't thinking about food. If I was going to be laying around after surgery, the temptations would be even bigger.

Food addicts canNOT have foods in their house that will trigger a relapse. Nobody questions it when a recovering alcoholic keeps no alcohol in the house, regardless of what others in the house want. The same must be true for food addicts. We saw this scenario play out on *Extreme Weight Loss* again and again. When a spouse or other child keeps junk around, the food addict struggles.

I was so blessed to have an accountability team that understood this reality or I wouldn't have made it through to my next goal at 9 months that earned me skin removal surgery. To this day, my home does not have chips, sweets, or unhealthy foods.

....

People came along with me on my weight loss journey in more ways than being on my accountability team. Part of my integrity meant that I had to be a leader for them. My mother lost more than 70 pounds at 70 years of age! She weighed in every Friday and would call me to prove she had been keeping track.

My dad still has to come around, but he's proud of Mom and me and didn't stand in the way of our progress. My sister also needs to make healthier choices. I will be there in the stands, rooting for her, as she rooted for me for so many years. Changes are coming though. I, of all people, know it's a slow learning process.

At church, where food is often the center of activity, I am trying to be a voice of healthy choices, too.

As for my amazing wife, Kelly, she's been right there with me! Even while she was in recovery from her kidney donation (and always smokin' hot, in my opinion anyway) she managed to successfully take off 50 pounds and now has a personal trainer certification. (It's my dream that we can work together in the future to bring that message of whole health—mind, body, and soul—to organizations that desperately need this foundation today!)

My son, Jordan, also did workouts with me and was a great supporter of everything that this final part of my transformation could mean for our family. Then, there was my first born.

Kayla is my parents' goddaughter. When Kayla was born, we asked them to be godparents. We couldn't think of anyone who loved her more, besides us of course. There isn't a thing in the world that can take away that utter, fulfilling elation of becoming a parent. Maybe that's why nothing is more disappointing than when you feel like you haven't succeeded in parenthood.

I remember when the film crew came to the house and asked my family how things were going. It's their job to tell the whole story surrounding the cast member. They invested in me and wanted to share the most dramatic pieces of my story with their viewing audience. Don't take this as an insult to the producers. They're really gifted at what they do, especially Matt Assmus and his team, including Brandon Roberts, Kerry Shanahan and Jason Kemppainen.

The stories these off-camera artists ultimately create are the same true, inspirational tales that motivate people across the country to take weight loss journeys of their own. They know what they're doing. Millions watched my episode and shared such undeserved gratitude. That gratitude is for the on- and off-camera talent of *Extreme Weight Loss*, too.

The drama in my house was pretty quick to spot. My then 19-year-old daughter served it up in the form of not wanting to be a part of all the changes I chose. To be fair, Kayla wasn't raised in the church and certainly not with healthy habits. She knew the 450-pound, long-hour-working, scruffy-looking, drinking, man's man ... not the family man. Kayla was around for bankrupt accounts and emotional bankruptcy. She was there for all the fights between her mom and me and dozens of small loss/ large gain crash diets.

When Kayla said she thought it was unfair that we all had to eat "health food" even though this

It was great to have the support of my daughter at my finale. We have tried to support our kids by encouraging a healthy lifestyle. Kayla has been doing some training with John Pietenpol.

was MY thing, the show knew they had a story. They even asked my daughter if she was okay with them taping her when she had her conversation with me about the perceived injustice of not being able to have fast food. It was her choice, and I was worried about how she would be portrayed, but she wanted to be honest.

I understood the skepticism Kayla felt. I feel a lot of guilt over not being the best leader in my home for many years. But, she got to see the finale with close up eyes and as a fan.

She was there for all the great moments, and I showed her as best as I could that transformation can be real. Kayla asked us to pay for CrossFit for her, but I told her she didn't need that. We told her she could use our home gym, work out with her brother, and go back to school while living with us.

Kelly and I want to give our daughter a successful path, but she needs to make the decision to step onto it. It's time. Kayla needs to be able to put forth the hard work and effort, and I know her success will come.

"This is what it takes," I told her. "I want to guide you as a father." I wish I had begun as this leader so much sooner than I did.

Kayla is not a girl who can be pushed. She is her mother's and father's daughter, no doubt, but I have both told her and shown her that I want health for her.

I want my dad to be healthy, like my mom, who worked hard with me through my transformation.

I want my sister, Becky, to join me at one more game, just as she did all those years she supported me in my sports. This game is for keeps though. Fitness. Nutrition. Health.

I want my church community to begin to honor their bodies as the Bible says we should.

I want to be a leader, with my wife, in whole health.

I want to see businesses and organizations run in ways that are healthy from the inside out.

Of course, more than anything, I want my kids to be well and to choose the healthy life decades before I chose it for myself with Kelly's help. I want them to have lives of exercise and good dietary choices … lives of integrity.

It's up to individuals to make the commitment, but I am more than willing to be the love, just as God provided those to love me through my own transformation.

Transformation: Strength!

Lifting weights may seem intimidating or confusing to people who do not work out or are new to the gym. Incorporating weight lifting into a regular exercise program has many purposes [...]:

- *Building Muscle*
- *Losing Weight*
- *Mental Health*
- *Anti-Aging*

**~*What Is the Purpose of Lifting Weights?*
by: Gabrielle Nicolet, Demand Media**

Transformation *takes* Strength! I remember starting out with my training, and what killed me most of all was, quite frankly, my fatness! Moving those 400 plus pounds made it work just to complete everyday tasks, so a workout was exhausting at best.

My muscles were tired.

There were times I felt like my lungs would explode.

I remember having to burp because I felt sick.

Dealing with the physical aspects of being so heavy was so hard on my muscles during the early phase of my transformation. In my mind, I was still that athlete, but I couldn't do things like an athlete because I was so heavy!

The good thing about having to move all that weight around, though, is that my muscles were working very hard.

You NEED muscles for everyday, functional living. I knew what it was to not be able to do the tasks that everybody around me was taking for granted:

- **Bend Over to Pick Up a Bag of Groceries**
- **Tying Shoes**
- **Lifting a Gallon of Milk**

Once I moved on from my own body being my strength training, I added weight training back into my workouts. When you're younger or involved in sports, you may choose to bulk up, but a person can really only add so many pounds of pure muscle to a body in a year, and that number shrinks as you age. Often people are afraid to incorporate strength training because they fear getting big. Weight training is about more than bulking up. It is also for:

- **Toning**
- **Strengthening**
- **Fat Burning**
- **Enjoyment**

The more muscles a person engages in a workout, the more calories that person will burn—it's science. Also, nobody is expecting everybody to have a set of dumbbells, bars, benches, kettle balls, or weighted balls. These things are great tools, but weight training can be done with any number of things that are kept right around the house, including:

- **Soup Cans**
- **Books**
- **Backpacks**
- **Water Jugs or Milk Gallons**

It was important to me to incorporate strength training because I wasn't just trying to get small with my weight transformation. I was trying to get healthy. I was trying to get STRONG.

- **Strength Train for Functional Living**
- **Strength Training Does Not Mean Bulking Up**
- **Use the Tools You Have to Strength Train**

Never forget that true transformation will give a person ...
... *strength.*

F.aith in God

For every child of God defeats this evil world, and we achieve this victory through our faith.

~1 John 5:4 (NLT)

Once I'd made the commitment to be the person I could love, I learned to be the person who could honor the love of others. I found the integrity to stick to my commitments, but I still struggled with how to possibly mount this C.L.I.F. How would I make it through all 250 plus pounds one at a time?

That's where faith came in. Faith was my new "F" in C.L.I.F.

CHRIS SAYS

"I told him transformation requires a leap of faith. It's terrifying when you simply do it. But, it's the most eye-opening experience in the world because you learn to understand yourself on so many different levels— physically psychologically, spiritually ... everything. Especially when it comes to integrity, and falling without failure, and understanding the emotional side. That's always the stuff that's brought to the table early on in the transformation. Heidi didn't have that much to do on that side. He came ready. He had the courage to be open and honest during the entire process, and that's the hardest part ... it's not just diet and exercise."

Chris's "falling without failing" is a theme that great athletes and leaders have used for generations. Vince Lombardi, a coach that even a Bear fan could admire, famously said that it doesn't matter how many times you get knocked down but how many times you get back up. My faith in God gave me the strength and courage to endure that year of exercising three hours a day, eating properly, cutting alcohol, and avoiding fast food … to keep getting back up. It sustained me. Faith kept me centered. It centered me from the very start. There were times I was in the middle of a workout, and I was overcome with emotions because I truly felt blessed at how great God was.

Another of the devotionals that touched me from Sarah Young's *Jesus Today* book really spoke to my gratefulness and my feeling of being blessed. It read:

> *Thankfulness is not some sort of magical formula. It is the language of love, which enables you to communicate intimately with me. A thankful mindset does not entail a denial of reality with its plethora of problems. Instead, it rejoices in me, your Savior, in the midst of trials and tribulations. I am your refuge and strength and ever-present and well-proved help in trouble.*

I had been in trouble, and God was well proven. I didn't feel worthy enough, but I didn't need to be worthy. I was already blessed. I had been shown so much grace, and it was powerful. That's what faith means to me.

Faith needed to be something that would fulfill me, not just something that filled the moment, that filled your stomach, or that filled a lust or desire.

I was all in.

I was ready to believe that God would fill my soul enough to sustain me through life's hardest trials. Even more than the incredible fitness team I had in John, Chris, and Heidi, this was what got me through the workouts and the temptations.

HEIDI SAYS:

> *"Bob always got his reward from more than just the weight loss. He understood that transformation wasn't just about weight loss."*

Through Chris Powell, I was able to have an understanding of my food addictions. An addict is an addict. You chase that thing that satisfies. For a food addict, you get that fulfillment from flavor and that "full" feeling. When you start to work out, addiction doesn't go away. Most people replace the food addiction with an addiction to the endorphin release from physical fitness. A few get their highs by playing the numbers game. They see that numbers drop and feel adrenaline rise.

The only way I was going to beat my addiction was to replace it with a target that could always be achieved. My satisfaction, my addiction, was fed by chasing the integrity and chasing the commitment. I reached them by holding onto faith.

My faith had seen me through much harder obstacles than nutrition and fitness.

....

Kelly staying ...

"I was probably ready to pull the plug on the marriage and walk away three or four times. For some reason, I couldn't. I don't know why. Fear? I was there, but I never did it even when I thought I could not do it one more day.

He never had that feeling. Never. It was me. But, had Paul not had that initial conversation, I don't think we'd be here today.

This was something that had to happen because he was prideful, driven by things that most people get caught up in, and we were in financial ruin. Things weren't right. We weren't talking unless we were at each other. It was a whole combination of things. But those things happen for a reason.

Now, looking back, I realize we had to go through them to come out to where we are now. We had to rely on each other at the base of everything."

....

And, in Kelly's letter that she shared while we were in France, she recognized that faith was the glue that held us together, as well as what pushed me through the transformation.

"... I thank God every day that you opened your heart to a conversation with HIM. Without you making a conscious decision to explore your relationship with Him, I'm not sure where we would be here today."

I learned that I didn't actually have to be fit, fixed, or transformed to be changed. I only need to be surrendered. God did the rest. I was an obese man when I chose to go under the water for my baptism. I knew that God would help me to become the man He needed me to be from there.

My new climb was Commitment.

My new climb was Love.

My new climb was Integrity.

My new climb was Faith.

At the beginning of my journey, I could only see the step in front of me. Now, with a leap of faith, it was the finish line up ahead.

KELLY SAYS:

"It's gonna keep this time. Partly because his mind and his heart are right at the same time. He's not the prideful, selfish person he was before. He prays every day and reaches out to accountability partners."

....

One of the things the Christian community doesn't do very well is that they give all sorts of pats on the back because *"Hey! God loves you just the way you are!"* Of course that's true, but the second part of that when a person is not living up to a full, healthy potential is, *"Hey! What you're doing, though, is not God's plan."*

RiverGlen Christian Church did a good job of respecting my privacy throughout my weight loss transformation, but they also supported me and allowed me to share my journey. I was surrounded by accountability in this environment where my only chance of reaching others was to be true to my own commitments.

A lot of people who lose weight, and especially once television and media get involved, will do anything to get from Point A to Point B. I made lifestyle changes. I didn't take weight loss pills. I used diet and exercise. It was repeatable. When it's true commitment, it needs to be a well-rounded plan, and that helped me stick to it, along with help from my local area trainer, John.

I shared with John that I had to make other changes, too. In my coaching, it was common for the adults to go out for a couple of beers after a game. Those couple of beers turned into a lot of beers, and a lot of beers turned into bad food decisions. I had to separate myself from that environment for a while. Now, I have the willpower, but it took some time to build that.

At the end of my weight transformation, John gave me a wonderful gift. He told me I could have free training for life at Revolution Fitness. If he ever starts to see the scale begin to creep back up, he tells me, "You're gonna lose your membership!" John keeps me accountable.

JOHN SAYS:

> "I just want to keep Bob coming here. He's given me a gift. He helped me realize what I want to do with my LIFE!
>
> Most of my clients want to lose a little bit of weight or they're already in shape and just maintaining (which is Bob today), but to make a real difference is pretty awesome. I want to continue to work with the very overweight and obese and Bob helps. Sometimes, it's nice to have a person here who can answer the question, 'How did you do it?'
>
> And you can really tell that Bob has changed. I mean really changed. When we worked together the first time, he came back with those extra 100 pounds and said that he didn't understand how it happened. He didn't have integrity then. He does today. People really respond to him, and he's changed the gym by being here. He bought into the whole package."

When I found faith, that was the piece that put it all together. You can take a leap of faith even when you don't know where it will lead because you have hope that it will lead to somewhere better than where you are. Faith is hope in the promise of God to honor those who honor Him.

John and I each had a goal for the other. His was to get me to lose the weight. Mine was to get him to church. John helped see me through the last part of my transformation … his goal for me. It was a transformation that would open up countless additional possibilities for serving the greater good. Health through faith is my new mission field. John is already in it with me. As for church … tell you what, John. I'll give you free membership for life.

Transformation: Stretch!

Tips to Reduce Injury Doing Yoga (adapted from WebMD):

- *Don't try learning yoga without an experienced instructor.*

- *Know what your limits are and respect them.*

- *Start with the basics and take it slow.*

- *Be sure to warm up first. Cold muscles are more likely to get injured.*

- *Wear clothing that doesn't restrict your movement.*

- *Drink lots of water.*

- *Listen to your body. If it's painful, don't do it.*

Transformation *requires* a person to stretch. You will run into obstacles on the way to your goals. Just like Ben shared in his sermon message at the start of my year of weight transformation, "In this world, you will have trouble." It wasn't just about fighting my own demons, the addictions, and the self-hate. I had actual, physical problems, too.

The show documented my knee problems well. It was a real setback. I had to basically stay static during a lot of exercises early on. No jumping. No twisting. It wasn't until I was under

300 pounds that I was able to start doing jumps or burpees and, even then, it was small. My knees just hurt.

All.

The.

Time.

My injuries were from the stress and strain I had put on my joints during years of being lined up in a half-squat on a football line, only to spring off of it and slam my body into solid walls of strong men. I was past lying to myself though. Of course my morbid obesity exacerbated my injuries.

The knees kept me from the jumps and twists in the beginning of my weight loss. Later in my year, I had to have the surgery on those knees I was finally healthy enough to undergo. That took me out of the cardio game for a while. When you get skin removal surgery at the nine-month mark, you can control your weight loss ONLY through your diet. There will be no exercising during that time if you don't want to destroy incredible stitch work.

HEIDI SAYS:

> *"I know it was hard for Bob to just stop working out after all that time. It wasn't in his nature to quit. He had come so far. It was hard for him to take the break his body needed to recover from surgery."*

Worst of all is the normal, everyday, every BODY stuff. I had weeks when I would lose only a couple of pounds, or just one, and a week when I didn't lose anything. It happens. I had to throw my body an occasional curveball. I needed to be flexible. I needed to stretch my workout repertoire. I needed to just plain stretch.

Hot yoga became a part of my routine. My knees felt best when I did yoga. The stretching and strengthening poses, in a 105-degree room, helped the muscles around the joints. For me, yoga was threefold:

- **The Sweating was Great for Weight Loss.**
- **The Pores of My Skin Opened Up for a Clearer Complexion.**

- **I Had 90 Minutes of Not Having to Talk or Think. My Mind Wandered and I was Able to Focus on Me and God.**

Transformation taught me to …
… *stretch.*

.

C.L.I.F. Notes

I came into the latest chapter of my life as a very large, yet very broken man. I knew it was time for a change, so I made decisions about what my new life pillars would be. I used to believe in my game, my work, my buddies, my fun, and, above all, my image. Not one of these pillars was strong enough to hold up my frame.

When I turned my belief to God and to the leaders and lessons HE provided, that frame didn't have to be held up anymore. I was strengthened from the inside—a solid structure built on COMMITMENT, LOVE, INTEGRITY, and FAITH. It is through this new person that I was able to make my climb. The reason I was able to experience and bring to the world my weight transformation is because I'd already been given the gift of a life transformation.

I know there are people who want to hear the tips and lists related to my time on *Extreme Weight Loss,* and I have tried to sprinkle those honest lifestyle changes into my story. Use them! They *will* help. I truly am grateful for the fact that I was chosen for the show, but I need the world to understand that my reality didn't fall into place on reality television. Chris and Heidi Powell will always be a part of my life, but it is the God I chose before they chose me that put them into my path at all.

Theme: Belief is Everything for Me

I didn't make it through my year of weight transformation alone. Doing it on my own was about fast diets, followed by fast foods, followed by fast diets, followed by fast foods. It was a vicious cycle, and I needed my transformation to be about more than the numbers on the scale. When my belief in God became the center of my world, my belief in what I could accomplish through that God fell naturally into place.

I want to impress upon everybody I can touch with my message of climbing the C.L.I.F. that it doesn't have to be hard. The problem most people have with commitment is that they are often setting themselves up for failure. A commitment doesn't have to be going to the gym for several hours every day or even for 45 minutes every day.

It is said that every obese person gains their weight one pound at a time.

Guess what.

It comes off the same way.

Instead of trying to tackle the whole line, I used to hit the guy in front of me. This was no different. I had to make realistic commitments and set realistic expectations. When just starting out, maybe commit to walking to the stop sign and back on weekdays. The important part comes in honoring that commitment … in honoring the promises we make to ourselves.

When I honored my commitments, my self-esteem and self-worth grew. I felt good about myself because I made the commitment and I succeeded. Then, I made another commitment. And another. I started living as God intended, and life just kept getting better. Start with those small commitments. Here are a few that became lifestyle changes for me.

Lessons in Commitment:
- **Get 8 hours of sleep.**
- **Be more active—get out and do more.**
- **Share activities with those you love for enjoyment of the activity and bonding with the loved one.**
- **Perform acts of service and kindness to others because it's good for the soul to do nice things.**

- Have positive people around you.
- Find a purpose to what you are doing.
- Keep your faith in God strong.
- Limit your screen time.
- Limit your alcohol.
- Do things outside of your comfort zone.

When it comes to commitment, the real C.L.I.F. Note lesson is to keep those commitments. The number one commitment I made was on November 13, 2010, when I committed to follow a God much bigger than even I was.

> Commitment means to plan well and follow through.
> I understand the priorities necessary for setting my commitments.
> I desire to be committed to those who committed so much to me.

Symbolism: Leap of Faith with Me

Loving yourself is a hard thing to do, even when there's a lot to love. This is where God really helped me. God did love me, even at 448 pounds, so I knew there was something worth saving and somebody worth serving. Through Him, I became a better man who benefitted by gaining the undeserved love of those around me.

God tells us in Matthew 10:29–31 (NLT),

> What is the price of two sparrows—one copper coin? But not a single sparrow can fall to the ground without your Father knowing it. And the very hairs on your head are all numbered. So don't be afraid; you are more valuable to God than a whole flock of sparrows.

You should look in the mirror and love that person that you see. If you don't love yourself, look to that love from others. The love you receive through friendships, family, community, and God can be how you learn to love yourself.

Lessons in Love:
- **You matter.**
- **You have value.**

So many times, the people around us in our lives want more for us than we want for ourselves. Certainly my wife did. My children did. My God did. When it comes to Love, the real C.L.I.F. Note lesson is that if you can't find the love in yourself, you need to start with the love from others.

> *Love means to love others. It starts by loving yourself.*
> *I understand that I have worth and therefore am capable of love.*
> *I desire to show every person, of every size, that they deserve love.*

Lifestyle: Rejoicing on the C.L.I.F.

With the love of those around me, integrity became a much easier principle to uphold. It was impossible for me to look at the woman of my life, and of my dreams, without wanting to return love to her. I wanted to express honesty to Kelly by keeping my promises to her. I wanted to express strength to her by keeping my promises to myself and being a good leader for our home. Most of all, I wanted to be around for her.

My newfound integrity led to greater blessings, not just in my marriage, but in all my relationships and in my life.

Lessons in Integrity:
- **Keep your promises to yourself.**
- **Keep your promises to others.**

When it comes to integrity, the real C.L.I.F. Note lesson is that keeping promises is a new choice to be made with every new promise. Fulfilled promises become fulfilled blessings.

> *Integrity means following through, even if nobody is watching.*
>
> *I understand that I used to be a different person for friends and family.*
>
> *I desire to be my best me for the woman I love.*

Character Insight:
About Growing My World

When I was young, I used to have goals about getting to the best game, getting to the best party, getting with the best girl, and getting the best job. Those weren't bad goals ... well, maybe except for the unnecessary partying. The point was that these were all checklist items I thought I needed to be a fulfilled person.

I only needed to check ONE thing off my list: Get to the Best ME. And I got to the best me through a loving God who believed in, and made, an even better me.

Lessons in Faith:
- **Believe in a better hope.**
- **Believe in a better future.**
- **Believe in a better ... YOU.**

When it comes to faith, the real C.L.I.F. Note lesson was to stop trying to be an image and to start trying to be me. I surrendered to a power bigger than I had been at my biggest. I surrendered to a life of COMMITMENT, LOVE, INTEGRITY, and FAITH. I was shown undeniable love, unending support, and an undeserved grace.

It's true that I was given a new body for my new life, but it's also true that ... *it's not about the weight.*

> *Faith means you don't need to know the whole path; just the next step.*
> *I understand that I can only control my own choices.*
> *I desire to lead the ones I love on their own faith journeys.*

Extreme and Unstoppable
What They Mean While Growing My World

I had been extreme in every way I failed. I was extremely obese. I was extremely alcoholic. I was extremely cruel to the ones who poured the most into me while extremely gracious to a life that was dragging me down. My selfishness and pride were never unstoppable. I just didn't realize that there was a force strong enough to stop them—me—strengthened by God.

In this realization, I finally took my extremes to a place where I could make a difference in the world. I know that every role I've served has helped to equip me to serve in my next brotherhood … the brotherhood of man … wherein my lost weight will allow me to serve my gained purpose of bringing the message of COMMITMENT, LOVE, INTEGRITY, and FAITH to those who feel like they are fallen, broken, and beyond repair.

As my buddy Chris would say, "We need to learn to fall, without failing."

Applying the
C.L.I.F.

How One Man Is Using
Commitment, Love, Integrity,
and Faith in His Life

Ask around town, and you'll find it's hard to find too many people who don't know, or know of, Gregg Wandsneider. His brown, moppy head of hair falls over the thirty-six-year-old man's always smiling face. The Carroll College graduate can be spotted all about town doing any number of tasks, including:

- Becoming the Salvation Army volunteer of the year
- Receiving a community service award from the Freemasons
- Receiving a Rotary Club volunteer award
- Writing for the local paper, *The Waukesha Freeman*
- Volunteering as a student mentor for Carroll University
- Serving on the Spiritual Advisory Board of Carroll University
- Being a RiverGlen Children's Ministry volunteer leader
- Running three music and talk radio programs for local stations

On the surface, these are pretty cool tasks. Even Waukesha Mayor, Jeff Scrima, took notice and gave Gregg the key to the city in December 2013. He commended Gregg for writing about, "… the good, the true, and the beautiful … " in our town. These accomplishments become more impressive when you learn that Gregg Wandsneider, who also works with a number of local schools to address issues of bullying and self-esteem, has been blind since birth due to a misconnected optic nerve in his brain.

In September 2013, Gregg was among about two hundred people who attended a live viewing party for my Extreme Weight Loss episode. During commercials, I would answer questions or talk about some of the behind-the-scenes action that didn't make the final cut. Gregg sat there in the front row, and he broke into tears to tell me that he was feeling motivated to make a change.

There are three things that people will notice about Gregg when they meet him. The first, of course, is his blindness. When people see him around town, they realize that he is also a huge community supporter. Unfortunately, those who don't take the time to get to know him may just see the third thing: it's hard to look past Gregg's obesity.

GREGG SAYS:

> "In Bob's episode, he talked about how he was successful in all of these other parts of his life, but he just couldn't get past the weight thing. I related to that. I mean, how can I motivate myself to go into schools and the community, but I can't motivate myself to lose the weight? Bob talked about not being able to conquer that thing, and I felt the same way.
>
> I am an emotional person and I have been known to even cry at Full House episodes, but there is a difference between crying because I'm entertained and crying because I'm motivated. I felt motivated.
>
> The other thing that struck me was when Kayla came in with the fast food. My mom is always suggesting snacks

for me, and I turn my nose up at them because they're healthy. I don't want to do that anymore. I don't want to eat things that will harm me. I just don't want to expose myself to that.

This change has been in my heart for a long time. I've known that I need to make this change and I'm on medication for high blood pressure and high cholesterol. I don't want to be on these medicines.

This time, the change is provoked by both want AND need."

We're ALL worth it. I told Gregg that he was worth it. "I'm proud of you. It's a journey. You don't need to see the finish line, just the step in front of you," I told him.

Gregg made some initial steps. He joined a gym, got a trainer, and announced his intentions to lose ten pounds a month until he was healthy. It was clear that he was really making a commitment and not just moved in the immediate moment, so I wanted to be of help to him. For Gregg, one of the biggest issues was just getting some basic nutritional tips, especially as a man who spends a lot of time around town, frequenting the local restaurants. A few ideas I offered him include:

- **Talk to the restaurant to help you keep track of your calories. You can use free phone apps for chain restaurants, but at locally owned establishments, ask the staff.**
- **Limit any of your white flours. They include a ton of carbs and not a whole lot of good nutrients.**
- **Spinach, pecans, broccoli, and fruit are all great foods.**
- **Try to limit meat to five-ounce portions, especially when out. Ask for it without salt when you're eating out.**
- **Green vegetables can be consumed in almost unlimited amounts. You get your fiber there, and that will help you feel full.**
- **Potatoes and sweet potatoes are good for you, but make them medium, not large. Leave the skins on,**

and use garlic powder instead of salt and a spritz of spray butter instead of sour cream.

- Limit your fats to about a tablespoon a day. Good fats include almonds, walnuts, and avocado.
- A favorite for satisfying a sweet tooth craving is a 100-calorie cup of frozen Greek yogurt. It tastes like ice cream, and you won't feel as though you've failed.
- A banana at breakfast will also take care of a sweet tooth.
- If sweets are your downfall, allow this as your weekly flex-day treat. Have a half cupcake from one of the local cafes you enjoy.
- Dairy can be okay, but limit it, and get the most out of it that you can, nutritionally. This is why I use Greek yogurt.

Gregg also needed to understand that there is a lot to change and it's long-term … a whole new lifestyle. He got it and even shared with me the way that C.L.I.F. has come into play in his own life. Here are some of Gregg Wandsneider's applications of the C.L.I.F. approach!

Lessons in Commitment:
- I need to see the small steps as victories.
- I set a goal to get home earlier at night, so that I'm not doing late-night eating and can get enough rest.
- I have a cousin taking me to my gym sessions so that I have made the commitment not just to the gym, but to a person I care about.
- I paid in advance for gym membership and training sessions so that I have a financial obligation.

Lessons in Love:
- My good, Christian friends have shared concerns about my weight.
- My body is a holy temple.
- I choose not to do anything to harm God's temple.
- I want to be an example of God's love as long as possible, and I need to be healthy for that.

Lessons in Integrity:

- I need to feel good at the end of the day about who I am.
- I am accountable to all the people who are offering support and encouragement.
- I have a large sphere of influence, and I need to be an example to all those people.

Lessons in Faith:

- I want to use this as an opportunity to lead others to health.
- I want to inspire people.
- I need to change myself first. Then I can inspire other people, and I can show them that God did this for me.

Gregg has overcome obstacles in his way due to his blindness. In fact, he doesn't even desire to fix his blindness. When asked if he would choose to be cured if one was available, he says. "I don't know if it will ever be something that can be fixed and I don't care. I want the first face I ever see to be that of Jesus."

That's the attitude of somebody who wants real and meaningful life changes.

If Gregg Wandsneider, a blind, obese man, can do this, I don't see any limits to living a life on the C.L.I.F. Every positive choice he makes will help him in his climb! I'm so proud to know Gregg, and I am grateful to be able to help and follow his journey on a road paved with COMMITMENT, LOVE, INTEGRITY, and FAITH.

Gregg, you can do it, Buddy!

Photo courtesy of Gregg Wandsneider

Gregg may have learned the C.L.I.F. approach from me, but he taught me what it means to serve other people. Every single day of his life, he volunteers his time and energy to serve his community.

Get Extreme: Tips to Transform YOUR Life!

Give and you will receive. Your gift will return to you in full—pressed down, shaken together to make room for more, running over, and poured into your lap. The amount you give will determine the amount you get back.

~Luke 6:38 (NLT)

I know that a number of people I've met throughout the course of *Extreme Weight Loss*, as well as through my speaking events since my final weigh-in and the airing of my episode, are interested in starting their own journeys. They desire their own transformations and their own ascents up their own C.L.I.F.s. I knew when I began my weight loss that it wasn't something I'd do alone. I didn't do it alone on the show. I haven't maintained my new body alone since the show, and I don't want to stand alone on my C.L.I.F.

What follows are the tips you can incorporate into your own life in addition to an approach to goal setting that will help you *LOSE YOUR WEIGHT, GAIN YOUR PURPOSE,* and—like me—*INVITE OTHERS* on the journey. On top of the tips compiled throughout this book, you'll be asked to consider making C.L.I.M.B. goals in order to enable you to come alongside me in your transformation. C.L.I.M.B. goals will get you up your personal C.L.I.F.s, and they include the necessity of being C.ENTERED, L.OGICAL, I.NDEXED, M.OTIVATED, and B.ALANCED.

There is a lot of information here. A whole book is required for whole transformation after all. Instead of being overwhelmed by trying to implement *every* idea, choose one to three new habits to apply from each of the transformation areas, choose a lesson or two to help you balance your life, and choose a couple of people and products to aid you. Once you have those initial goals successfully implemented, add a couple more. It's an incremental process. It's not a race but a journey. I want to help you take that first step on your C.L.I.F.

What is a C.L.I.M.B. goal?

It is **C.ENTERED** on a specific task. In other words, these goals need to be very specific. If you have a goal to be a better person, for instance, that is too vague. Does that mean you need to live with better health decisions, make less impulsive spending choices, be more dedicated to relationships in your life, give more to charity, or something else entirely? You need to find a targeted life area on which to work. Make sure your goal is CENTERED.

Make goals that are **L.OGICAL**. Especially with weight objectives, it's very important that you take a realistic approach to the physical transformation. You'll notice I'll be recommending some products that helped me along in my weight loss. It was a hard decision to include these in my plan as I was nervous about the stigma surrounding the supplement industry and all of the products that do more harm than good. The line I ultimately chose to include is natural, healthy, and safe. As should be no surprise, not *all* products can make such a claim. Popping countless weight loss pills, using laxatives, and subjecting yourself to starvation diets are not healthy choices. And, it is not LOGICAL to set a goal to lose so much weight (in so short a time) that those gimmicks are the only way to make the achievement.

I.NDEX your goals as "milestones" along the way. Those milestones should have *measurable achievements* that must be reached by *predetermined times*. It's no accident that the members of the *Extreme Weight Loss* casts are given weigh-ins at three-month intervals throughout our year on the show. Those indexes are in place in order to maintain integrity and accountability. You must also have these things in place to keep your motivation, particularly if there are times when your why (see below) seems out of reach. The other thing you may notice about the milestone achievements I and others made on *Extreme Weight Loss* is that they changed. In the beginning, the amount of weight we had to lose was far greater than the amount we had to take off in the last three months (logic!). Lastly, when we reached indexes on our journey, we celebrated. Mark your achievement with a moment of recognition, while keeping your ultimate goal both results- and time-INDEXED.

M.OTIVATE yourself toward the WHY of your goal. Changes you make for the sake of change are not going to fulfill ... they won't satisfy. My weight loss journey, for instance, was not just about dropping pounds. It was important to me that I thought about all of the things that the weight loss meant. I would be around for my kids. I could better support my wife. I could serve my community. The number on the scale was never the carrot for me; it was the man I could be when the scale reached that number. What is your carrot? Make sure your goals are MOTIVATED.

B.ALANCED goals are vital to keeping all of the plates in your life spinning. If you set a goal that requires 100% of your time, then other areas of your life could suffer as a result. Remember when setting a weight loss goal *(or any goal for that matter)* to not neglect the people and reasons that make you want to lose the weight *(or achieve another objective)* in the first place. If I had chosen to spend my workout time separate from Kelly, my marriage might have suffered as a result. Instead, I included her, and together we both flourished and became healthier. The same is true for my faith. I could easily have made my fitness my new idol, but instead, I decided to use my faith to *help* move me through my transformation. C.L.I.M.B. goals are goals that help you maintain your BALANCE.

Example:
Short Goal: *"I want to be in better shape."*

> **C** — I need to lose fat and gain muscle.
>
> **L** — I want to lose 50 pounds over the next six months through a combination of exercises including strength training.
>
> **I** — I will weigh myself weekly and need to lose no less than 2 pounds per week.
>
> **M** — I have a reunion coming up, and I've been successful in my life, but nobody will see anything beyond my weight gain.
>
> **B** — I can include bike rides with my brother and walks with my wife to make sure I'm not cheating our quality time together.

New Goal: Over the next six months, I'll lose no less than 2 pounds per week through a combination of strength and cardio training and alongside my loved ones in order to appear on the outside as contented as I am on the inside.

You'll notice that all elements of a C.L.I.M.B. goal (CENTERED, LOGICAL, INDEXED, MOTIVATED, and BALANCED) are *interdependent*. A goal that is set with all five elements will be strong enough to hold you even when you feel yourself slipping on your C.L.I.F. When you set a C.L.I.M.B. goal, you'll be UNSTOPPABLE at reaching new heights … EXTREME heights!

•••••••••••••••••••••••••••

Lose Your Weight!

The following tips are from the *Transformation: Sweet!* and the *Applying the C.L.I.F.* chapters of this book where you can find additional and more detailed tips and applications to aid you in your transformation. Also, I have shared some of the Vemma® *(pronounced vē-ma)* products that I used throughout my *Extreme Weight Loss* journey and have continued to use in my weight maintenance since.

You'll notice that the tips regarding nutrition are far greater than those in any of the other *lose your weight* sections; this is because 70% of your physical transformation comes from what you put in your body and only 30% from the physical activity in which you partake with your body.

Tips for Nutrition:

- Drink 1/2 of your body weight in ounces of water per day.
- Allow yourself occasional treats ("flex day") without allowing over-indulgence.
- Limit (and count) your daily caloric intake.
- On your flex day, allow no more than a 40% increase in calories and ensure that the added calories are not all "empty."
- Have more daily meals of smaller average size.
- Treat cravings with:
  - a 12 oz. serving of water
  - a thumb's length of stacked almonds
  - your flex day indulgence
- Switch from traditional to Greek yogurt for:
  - 12 to 14 grams of protein
  - a longer lasting full sensation than traditional (mostly sugar) yogurts
  - a richer consistency to "fool the brain"
  - a longer digestive process that will keep you full longer
- Eat healthy on a budget through:
  - discount grocery stores
  - bulk buying of your staple foods
  - shopping seasonal and sale foods
  - stocking up on apples, bananas, and inexpensive filling fruits
  - replacing chicken breasts with thighs (remove the skin!)

- Do not have junk food in your house ... PERIOD.
- Devise a daily plan as well as a plan to deal with cravings, special occasions, and other expected bumps along the way.
- Vemma's® Bod-ē Cleanse (or comparable natural cleanse)
  - detoxes system with all natural, gentle, digestive regulation
  - includes fibers, whole grains, and metabolism boosters
- You can use free phone apps for nutritional information in chain restaurants, but at locally owned establishments, ask the staff.
- Limit any of your white flours. They include a ton of carbs and not a whole lot of good nutrients.
- Spinach, pecans, broccoli, and fruit are all great foods for nutritional density without caloric density.
- Try to limit meat to five-ounce portions, especially when out.
- Ask for foods without salt when you're eating out.
- Green vegetables can be consumed in almost unlimited amounts. You get your fiber there and that will help you feel full.
- Potatoes and sweet potatoes are good for you, but make them medium, not large. Leave the skins on, and use garlic powder instead of salt and a spritz of spray butter instead of sour cream.
- Limit your fats to about a tablespoon a day. Good fats include almonds, walnuts, and avocado.
- A favorite for satisfying a sweet tooth craving is a 100-calorie cup of frozen Greek yogurt. It tastes like ice cream, and you won't feel as though you've failed.
- A banana at breakfast will also take care of a sweet tooth.

- If sweets are your downfall, allow this as your weekly flex day treat: have a half cupcake from one of the local cafes you enjoy. (My flex day included a burger in a lettuce wrap at Red Robin ... very satisfying!)
- Dairy can be okay, but limit it, and get the most out of it that you can nutritionally. (This is why I use Greek yogurt.)

The following tips are from the *Transformation: Sweat!* chapter of this book where you can find additional and more detailed tips and applications to aid you in your transformation.

Tips for Cardiovascular Exercise:

- Monitor your effort and exhaustion levels—Consider using a heart rate monitor or other electronic measuring devices.
- Be willing to change your routine as your weight changes.
- Begin with low-impact workouts while you are still heavy to prevent damage to joints.
- Give your all to every workout—you've committed your time; now, commit your effort.
- If you don't belong to a gym:
    - Do hill repeats at a local park.
    - Pick up a used bike and hit the trails.
    - Use the internet to find free training videos.
    - Get workout DVDs from the local library.
    - Ask if your health insurance plan helps with (or has a discount for) gym plans.
    - Ask about gyms' financial assistance plans.
    - Know that people, in general, want to help; ask for it.
- In your home, you can do:
    - workout videos and programs

- abdominal training on a core ball
- sit-ups
- push-ups
- mountain climbers
- burpees
- planks
- Vemma's® Bod-ē Burn (*or comparable workout and electrolyte nutritional supplement*)
    - helps in pre- and post-workout nutrition
    - includes protein, vitamins, minerals, antioxidants, fiber, and an all-natural caffeine supplement
- Start according to your ability.
- Be flexible.
- Use the resources available to you.
- Make fitness a priority.
- Accept no excuses.

The following tips are from the *Transformation: Strength!* chapter of this book where you can find additional and more detailed tips and applications to aid you in your transformation.

Tips for Strength Training:

- Reasons to include strength training in a fitness regimen are:
    - building the right muscles
    - losing weight as you work your larger muscle groups
    - mental health balance
    - anti-aging effects from maintaining your skin and muscle shape
- Specifically, working with weights will help with:
    - toning

- strengthening
- fat-burning
- enjoyment from variety and accomplishment
- Strength train for basic functional living such as:
  - carrying groceries
  - tying shoes
  - getting in and out of vehicles
- You don't need weights; use what you have, including:
  - soup cans
  - water jugs
  - loaded backpacks
  - books
- Strength training does *not* mean *bulking up.*
- Vemma's® Bod-ē Shake *(or comparable protein-rich meal replacement)*
  - a great meal-on-the-go, especially when a workout is on the schedule
  - includes protein, soluble fiber, and a targeted amount of complex carbohydrates

The following tips are from the *Transformation: Stretch!* chapter of this book where you can find additional and more detailed tips and applications to aid you in your transformation.

Tips for Stretching, Resting, and Meditating:

- Try yoga in a hot room for:
  - increased burn from sweating
  - opened pores to clear your skin
- Vemma's® Bod-ē Rest *(or comparable caffeine-free, hydrating rest-inducer)*
  - helps an active body get the necessary rest at the end of a physical day

- includes patented Vemma® blend, no caffeine, and natural ingredients
- Stretch-style exercise is also great for:
  - meditation
  - self-focus
  - God-focus
- Stretch style will help to prevent and assist in recovery from:
  - injury
  - impact

....

Find Your Purpose!

When setting a C.L.I.M.B. goal, you wrap up your goal by focusing on BALANCE, on making sure that you don't lose sight of the people and reasons for which you are committing to a goal in the first place. If you wish to be in better health in order to be better at your job, it wouldn't do a lot of good to neglect your work while on your weight loss journey. This is why it's important to hold on to the lessons learned surrounding Commitment, Love, Integrity, and Faith. Here is a recap of those life lessons taken from the *C.L.I.F. Notes* chapters in the book, as well as from the *Applying the C.L.I.F.* chapter.

Lessons in Commitment:
- Take stock of the relationships you have.
- Take stock of why you have those relationships.
- Believe in the person you are, rather than the things you do.
- Commit to excellence in those relationships.
- Commit to the gifts you HAVE.
- Give time to what you value.
- Get 8 hours of sleep.
- Be more active—get out and do more.

- Share activities with those you love.
- Perform acts of service and kindness to others because it's good for the soul to do nice things.
- Have positive people around you.
- Find a purpose in what you are doing.
- Keep your faith in God strong.
- Limit your screen time.
- Limit your alcohol.
- Do things outside of your comfort zone.
- Set goals.
- See even small steps as victories.

Lessons in Love:

- Pay attention to who is looking up to you.
- Choose to be a character worthy of imitating.
- Remember words of love.
- Remember actions of love.
- You matter.
- You have value.
- Recognize your worth in your own belief system.
- Be an example of love.

Lessons in Integrity:

- Be honest with yourself.
- Strive to be more than an image.
- Recognize purpose.
- Put aside your ego.
- Keep your promises to yourself.
- Keep your promises to others.
- Feel good at the end of each day about who you are.
- Be accountable to all of those who are offering encouragement.

Lessons in Faith:

- Let go of trying to control everything.
- Accept that you can only be yourself.
- Trust that you have a purpose.
- There is always hope.
- Every person has worth.
- Believe in a better hope.
- Believe in a better future.
- Believe in a better ... YOU.
- Lead your sphere of influence.
- Inspire others.
- Change yourself first.

....

Invite Others

Transformation in the world happens when people are healed and start investing in other people.
~**Michael W. Smith**

Part of my purpose *is* the people. There are people in my life for whom I want to be better. There are people I meet to whom I wish to be an example of what whole-hearted transformation looks like. I have family to whom I want to show love and a church to whom I wish to show dedication. Most of all, though, I think about the people who helped me along in my journey. I wouldn't be here if it weren't for them.

A support system exists to cheer you on and celebrate when you make your milestones (the INDEXES in your goals). They are also there to give you a swift kick in the tail when you fall off the wagon. That's true accountability and you don't get to the finish line without it. You can design your own team but to try and make your C.L.I.M.B. without one would be ... well ... a heavy burden to carry. And, if you've picked up this book, just maybe you've had enough of that by now.

Here are some important people I suggest putting on your team in order to help make your C.L.I.M.B. a reality.

Partnered People:

- Your closest loved ones
    - Family: make sure they are on board with transforming your cupboards and home foods, too.
    - Friends: enlist them to join you on the journey through fitness events and by ordering healthy selections when you meet for meals.
- Experts in physical fitness and training
    - In person, you should build relationships with people who can help you implement fitness properly.
    - Feel free to use online experts, as well, but confirm credentials and take time to research the validity of the knowledge they share.
- Medical professionals
    - Check in with your physician throughout your weight loss in order to confirm that your heart, blood pressure, and other important statistics are not in danger.
    - You may require specialists for joints as you put new strains on long unused parts of your body.
    - Don't ignore the fact that you may have emotional issues as you transform, as well. You may need to speak with psychological professionals.
- Somebody who can relate
    - Don't lose weight alone. I had my "Three Amigos" and other cast members. They understood the journey and made it with me. Find somebody who can do that for you.

- Cheerleaders
    - We all need people who will hold the pom-poms, so to speak, to say, "You got this!" when we're feeling down.
- Tail-kickers
    - We also need people who will tell us to get going when we think it's too hard. Don't accept the words of those who will accept failure for you.
- Your employer and colleagues
    - When your place of employment is on board, you just might see an increase in fruit and vegetable trays and a decrease in doughnuts and cake brought in. Many of us spend as much time in our workplaces as our homes. Have them help perform the nutritional detox in the break room, just as your family performed a food makeover in your kitchen.
- Your community
    - Churches and organizations are great rallying points to keep you on track with your C.L.I.M.B. goals. If you have a community that's not particularly conducive to your new lifestyle, such as a group of "drinking buddies," those relationships may at least temporarily fall into the naysayers category (below).
- Your naysayers.
    - These people may even be your friends and family. You don't need to get them out of your life, but if they are not in line with your C.L.I.M.B. goals, share other parts of your life with them; they don't need to be a part of your transformation journey. Let them enjoy the results and pray that they come alongside you when you have seen through the program to a successful finish.

Ralph Waldo Emerson's famous words, *"our greatest glory is not in never failing, but in rising up every time we fall,"* have been shared in variations through many generations, including by my buddy, Chris. **Falling without failing** was a common mantra among the *Extreme Weight Loss* cast members. It's because of these words that I'm reminded of one other person or group you may need to bring alongside you in your transformation journey.

A large part of my obesity issue was related to addiction. In reality, I believe this is more common than not. I lived a life of addiction to food. Unfortunately, there is a certain reality to having an addictive personality. I was not only addicted to food but also to alcohol. Addictions often go hand in hand. It's easy to have more than one.

I am blessed that my church offers a group called *Celebrate Recovery*, which helps people deal with addiction as well as a number of other hurts, habits, and hang-ups. If your weight loss, or any other drastic life change you are making, includes a struggle with addiction, you may need to reach out to professionals to help you deal with the additional obstacles and issues that might arise as you work through your transformation. Consider seeking assistance through:

- **help-lines**
- **religious organizations**
- **recovery groups**
- **doctors, both medical and psychological**
- **online support communities**

....

In early 2014, I was asked to speak to the community of 10,000+ people involved in the Vemma® product line. It was an easy commitment to make. I have faith that their line is helpful and not harmful. I don't want to be a commercial, but I have promised to be fully honest with my readers throughout this book, so I want to lay it all on the table and tell you about the additional tools I used in my weight loss.

Do not think that just because this line is the one that I chose to use in my transformation, it is the only one out there. Ask *your* medical and training professionals about what, if any, products you could safely incorporate into your transformation plan. Be sure to consider the following:

- *Is the product sugar-free?*
- *Is the product natural?*
- *Is the product gluten-free?*
- *Are the ingredients simple or complex?*
- *What sort of research and science was involved in the product creation?*
- *Who do I trust that can attest to the product?*

I chose this line of supplements only after I was satisfied with answers to all of those questions. You should perform your own similar research.

Whole transformation requires a "whole self" approach. You need to consider, not just how to *lose the weight* but also how to *gain a purpose,* and who to help you along by *inviting others.*

One thing I learned over the past year since my episode ended is that healthy choices are truly a *lifestyle* that I needed to, and continue to, embrace. I love the Abraham Lincoln quote, *"The best thing about the future, is that it comes one day at a time."* I live every day with intention and purpose. That doesn't mean that I don't slip up from time to time. I do fall victim, on occasion, to my food addiction. However, I've learned to get back up. GETTING EXTREME is the comprehensive plan you can adopt to make you unstoppable and to learn how to fall without failing. Come C.L.I.M.B. with me … we have a C.L.I.F. to mount!

Be Active! **Take Action!**	

What changes do you need to make immediately for losing the weight, gaining your purpose, and inviting others? Write one for each area.

Set a short goal for one of the above changes:

Make it C.entered:

Make it L.ogical:

Make it I.ndexed:

Make it M.otivated:

Make it B.alanced:

What potential obstacles may exist while working toward your goal?

Restate your new CLIMB goal for change and include strategies to overcome potential obstacles:

As you accomplish each goal, create another! Consider using this CLIMB goal-setter worksheet as you reach toward each new change in all of your life areas.

Don't overwhelm yourself … take on no more than three goals at a time, and celebrate each win you achieve as you ascend life's C.L.I.F.!

Happy hiking, Buddy!
Bob

Unstoppable Transformation: Dropping the Fail from Your C.L.I.F.

We can rejoice, too, when we run into problems and trials, for we know that they help us develop endurance, and endurance develops strength of character, and character strengthens our confident hope of salvation. And this hope will not lead to disappointment. For we know how dearly God loves us ...

When Chris Powell announced the airing of my *Extreme Weight Loss* episode on his Facebook page, he told the world that I was the "UNSTOPPABLE BOB BRENNER!" Well, Buddy, I'm still not stopping!

BEN SAYS:

> *"As I've gotten to know Bob, I don't really see a limit. I don't see a barrier to him accomplishing anything, and that kind of excites me. I think God must have something big in mind for Bob."*

Chris led me on a one-year journey from almost 450 pounds to a stadium filled with an incredible support system and accountability team. He told me before the taping that I should just take it all in and, for that day, I did. I was so overwhelmed by the grace of God and the gift of the loves in my life that I couldn't really do much more than that. All the words I did try to form caught in my throat as I looked down at the Three Amigos, my church family, my folks and siblings, my kids and, most of all, my beautiful wife, glowing in the sunlight, her smile finally able to honestly show pride in me. Across her neck, sparkling against her bright top, is a golden symbol of what really brought us to this stage: the cross. I finally learned to love that woman in the way she deserved.

Stepping onto the scale (just a regular scale, not a commercial one), no matter what the number was, I knew I'd made it. The number didn't hurt to confirm it though. This time, unlike the nerves that filled me at my three-month weigh-in, six-month weigh-in, and nine-month weigh-in that resulted in successful skin removal surgery, I was calm. I was at peace … finally … comfortable in my skin and … *right where I was supposed to be*. The scale stopped chirping at 195 lbs. I had lost over 250 pounds in 365 days! 56% of my bodyweight had fallen off, yet I never felt more full!

I felt like I was on top of the world that day and I've felt like that ever since. I want everybody to know this feeling of utter completeness. I made the climb, and now, it's time for me to hold the ropes for as many people as I can so that they can come join me.

THIS is the new C.L.I.F. I want to ascend.

THIS is the new C.L.I.F. I want to invite as many people on as possible.

I want to live a life of Commitment, Love, Integrity, and Faith.

I want to live life with the God who loved me enough to teach me to love myself.

I lost my pride, but I gained Commitment, Love, Integrity, and Faith.

I lost growing myself, but through a transformed heart, transformed body, and transformed *life*, I get to help grow God's Kingdom.

I lost 250 pounds of emptiness to gain a purpose that begins with immeasurable

Photo courtesy of Kimberly Laberge

This is the picture of a redeemed man.

fullness in all the areas I had failed when I was trying to do it alone: my health, my addictions, my future, my faith, my relationships, and my LIFE.

Are you ready to join me in a leap of faith?

> *We can rejoice, too, when we run into problems and trials, for we know that they help us develop endurance, and endurance develops strength of character, and character strengthens our confident hope of salvation. And this hope will not lead to disappointment. For we know how dearly God loves us because he has given us the Holy Spirit to fill our hearts with his love.*
>
> **~Romans 5:3–5**

Are you ready to be all in?

God's son went all in for us on a cross on a hill—our part is easy.

Go all in on a leap of faith off a C.L.I.F. built on COMMITMENT, LOVE, INTEGRITY, and FAITH.

For, in this life, we *will* have problems, but we can rejoice too when we run into those problems.

Amen.

Acknowledgements

Simply put, *Live an Extreme Life* would not exist if not for the support of many wonderful individuals who helped it come together. We hope to remember them all here, but know that we hold them all in our hearts in a place of sincere gratitude.

First and foremost, to Bob Snodgrass, Chris Drummond, Rob Peters, Bob Ibach, Lenny Cohen, Dylan Tucker, and the Ascend Books team, thank you for believing in and taking on this project.

To editor, Katie Hoffman, your expertise in ironing out written details in this true life story has helped make a product of which we are proud.

To the families of Bob Brenner and Reji Laberje, particularly their respective spouses, Kelly and Joe, your cheerleading in our lives and for this project are invaluable. To Jordan, Kayla, Bradley, Kimberly, and Laura, the time we gave up to work on *Live an Extreme Life* came from you. Thank you.

To the two biggest communities responsible for affecting Bob's transformation, RiverGlen Christian Church and *Extreme Weight Loss*, you helped make this life change possible, and our appreciation is beyond words.

To the Waukesha Sheriff's Department, who allowed the flexibility to make *Extreme Weight Loss* and this book a possibility, we'll always have your back!

To John Pietenpol and the Revolution Fitness staff, thank you for your support in and out of the gym.

To Chris and Heidi Powell, Bonnie Schroader, and the Powell team, your assistance has been appreciated; your friendship is more like family, and your lessons will live on, transformed by faith.

To ALL of the on- and off-camera talent of *Extreme Weight Loss*, including, but not limited to, Matt Assmus, Kerry Shanahan, and the ENTIRE Season 3 cast, with particular thanks to Mike Epstein, Mehrbod Mohammadi, Jason and Rachel Cornellier, and Chantell Johnson, know that you are lifetime friends and an irreplaceable lifetime accountability team!

To all of those who provided valuable time and words through interviews, including, Bob Brenner, Sr. and Barbara Brenner, Kelly and Jordan Brenner, Bruce Brenner, Becky (Brenner) Urban, Paul Paikowski, Rob Hall, John Pietenpol, Chris and Heidi Powell, Ben Davis, John Howard, Steve Widmer, and Gregg Wandsneider, your storytelling has allowed for the bigger story to be told.

Thank you, also, for the written words of Chris Powell, Heidi Powell, Chantell Johnson, Mehrbod Mohammadi, Mike Epstein, Rachel Cornellier, Jason Cornellier, Cassandra Dumas, Stacy Rozmarynowski, and Felicia Froschmayer.

To the countless organizations that have opened their doors to hearing this story through Bob's new coaching and motivational speaking business, i Coach Transformation, LLC., we wish we had room to list you all. We hope you will always feel the enduring appreciation we have for the opportunity to share the secrets of transformation with your churches, families, corporations, organizations, and friends, and we look forward to continued work with you.

To the many who have provided photographic opportunities and photo contributions, including Andy Drefs, Rob Sims Studios, Kimberly Laberge, John Pietenpol, Leslie Sheen Wanasek, BTrick Photography, The Mangold Creative Team, Mike Epstein, Rob Hall, Barbara Brenner, Charity Miller, Kayla Brenner, and Kelly Brenner, a picture tells a thousand words— thank you for creating infinite stories.

To the many featured in true life anecdotes throughout this book: family, friends, teachers, coaches, pastors, colleagues, crews, and more, thank you for being a part of this blessed life.

To each and every one of you, this story can now be yours—a story of physical, emotional, mental, and spiritual redemption and transformation. It is our prayer that these words help you in your journey up the C.L.I.F. to live extreme, unstoppable lives in the most beautiful and blessed ways possible.

MOST of all, to a God who saw this all come together long before any of us ... we give our unending gratitude.

Bibliography

"Coach." *Merriam Webster Online.* Merriam Webster, 2014. Web. 6 Jan. 2014.

Cosby, Bill. *Fatherhood.* Garden City, NY: Doubleday, 1986. Print.

Davis, Ben. "Adversity." Stumbling onto Happiness Series. RiverGlen Christian Church, Waukesha, Wisconsin. 20 May 2012. Sermon.

"Extreme." *Merriam Webster Online.* Merriam Webster, 2014. Web. 6 Jan. 2014.

Extreme Weight Loss Season 03 Episode 13. Prod. Matt Assmus. Perf. Chris Powell and Bob Brenner. IWerks Entertainment, Inc., 2013. Television Broadcast.

"Family." *Merriam Webster Online.* Merriam Webster, 2014. Web. 6 Jan. 2014.

Hirn, Mike. "Weight Loss and Sweating It Off." *Ezine Articles.* EzineArticles. com, 19 Sept. 2006. Web. 24 Jan. 2014.

Lucado, Max. *A Gentle Thunder: Hearing God through the Storm.* Nashville: Word Pub., 1995. Print.

Lyubomirsky, Sonja. *The How of Happiness: A Scientific Approach to Getting the Life You Want.* New York: Penguin, 2008. Print.

Nicolette, Gabrielle. "What Is the Purpose of Lifting Weights?" *Healthy Living.* HealthyLiving.azcentral.com, n.d. Web. 24 Jan. 2014.

Rose, Brent. "The Science of Fat." *Gizmodo.* Fitmodo, 02 Feb. 2014. Web. 09 Feb. 2014.

"Trainer." *Merriam Webster Online.* Merriam Webster, 2014. Web. 6 Jan. 2014.

"Unstoppable." *Merriam Webster Online.* Merriam Webster, 2014. Web. 6 Jan. 2014.

Wigmore, Ann. Ann Wigmore Institute. Ann Wigmore Natural Health Institute, n.d. Web. 24 Jan. 2014.

"Yoga Health Benefits: Flexibility, Strength, Posture, and More." *WebMD.* WebMD, 28 Apr. 0011. Web. 24 Jan. 2014.

Young, Sarah. *Jesus Calling: Enjoying Peace in His Presence: Devotions for Every Day of the Year.* Nashville: Integrity, 2004. Print.

About the Authors

Bob Brenner is a police detective and former football player and coach. After an athletic youth left his body injured and exhausted, he spent the first 19 years of his adulthood letting himself go and letting himself grow. With the help of his church, he put his insides back together, and with the help of reality television and celebrity fitness trainer, Chris Powell, he put his outsides back together. Today, living outside of Milwaukee, Wisconsin, with his two children, his enormous dog Walter (Payton), and

Me with my co-author and friend, Reji Laberje.

Photo courtesy of Kimberly Laberge

his wife of more than 20 years, Kelly, Bob is successfully running his own life coaching and motivational speaking business. Bob inspires people to lives of whole health through his story of emotional, spiritual, and physical redemption. Learn more at **www.icoachtransform.com.**

Reji Laberje is a writer and speaker who has presented literary programming to thousands since 1997. She's an author of many books, including *Getting a W in the Game of Life,* written with ESPN's Dick Vitale, and the soon-to-be-released Max Plays board book series featured in children's museums around the country. Additionally, Reji writes fiction and inspirational nonfiction for elementary and young adult audiences, and she helps to craft material for professional speakers on the subjects of finance, health, success, and motivation. Reji lives with her husband of 18 years, Joe, and their three children (and four pets) near Milwaukee, Wisconsin. Learn more at **www.rejilaberje.com.**